Financial and Managerial Accounting or Managerial Accounting

THIRTEENTH EDITION

Carl S. Warren

Professor Emeritus of Accounting
University of Georgia, Athens

James M. Reeve

Professor Emeritus of Accounting
University of Tennessee, Knoxville

Jonathan E. Duchac

Professor of Accounting
Wake Forest University

W9-AZT-259

CENGAGE
Learning

Australia • Brazil • Mexico • Singapore • United Kingdom • United States

ISBN: 978-1-285-86959-9

Cengage Learning
5191 Natorp Boulevard
Mason, OH 45040
USA

Cengage Learning is a leading provider of customized learning solutions with office locations around the globe, including Singapore, the United Kingdom, Australia, Mexico, Brazil, and Japan. Locate your local office at: **www.cengage.com/global**.

Cengage Learning products are represented in Canada by Nelson Education, Ltd.

To learn more about Cengage Learning Solutions, visit **www.cengage.com**.

Purchase any of our products at your local college store or at our preferred online store **www.cengagebrain.com**.

Printed in the United States of America
2 3 4 5 6   20 19 18 17 16

CONTENTS

PREFACE

The working papers include problem-specific forms for preparing solutions for Exercises, A&B Problems, the Continuing Problem, and the Comprehensive Problems from the textbook. These forms, with preprinted headings, provide a structure for the problems, which will help you get started and save you time.

Based on students' testimonials and instructors' feedback, the forms in the working papers have been streamlined to make them simpler to use and to better reflect the changing environment of business. For example, the vertical rules that separated digits of numbers entered into journals, ledgers, and statements have been removed, making it easier to write in numbers.

Note that when entering whole amounts into the forms, your instructor will direct you on whether to include a decimal point and zeroes (e.g., 100.00) or to omit those (e.g., 100).

EXERCISE 16-1

a. Depreciation of robotic assembly line equipment: _____

b. V8 automobile engine: _____

c. Steering wheel: _____

d. Wheels: _____

e. Painting safety masks for employees working in the paint room: _____

f. Salary of test driver: _____

g. Glass used in the vehicle's windshield: _____

h. Wages of assembly line worker: _____

EXERCISE 16-2

a. Plant manager salary for the Iowa City, Iowa, plant: _____

b. Maintenance supplies: _____

c. Salary of process engineers: _____

d. Wages paid to Packaging Department employees in the Bear River City, Utah, paper products plant:

_____

e. Scents and fragrances used in making soaps and detergents: _____

f. Wages of production line employees at the Pineville, Louisiana, soap and detergent plant: _____

_____

g. Depreciation on assembly line in the Mehoopany, Pennsylvania, paper products plant: _____

_____

h. Packaging materials: _____

i. Resins for body wash products: _____

j. Depreciation on the Auburn, Maine, manufacturing plant: _____

EXERCISE 16-3

a. Plant manager's salary at Buffalo, New York, stamping plant, which manufactures auto and truck

subassemblies: _____

b. Depreciation on Flat Rock, Michigan, assembly plant: _____

c. Dividends paid to shareholders: _____

d. Machine lubricant used to maintain the assembly line at the Louisville, Kentucky, assembly plant:

_____

e. Leather to be used in vehicles that have leather interiors: _____

f. Depreciation on mechanical robots used on the assembly line: _____

g. Consultant fees for a study of production line efficiency: _____

h. Dealership sales incentives: _____

i. Vice president of human resources's salary: _____

j. Property taxes on the Detroit, Michigan, headquarters building: _____

EXERCISE 16-4

a. Research and development costs: _____

b. Depreciation on sewing machines: _____

c. Fabric used during production: _____

d. Depreciation on office equipment: _____

e. Advertising expenses: _____

f. Repairs and maintenance costs for sewing machines: _____

g. Salary of production quality control supervisor: _____

h. Utility costs for office building: _____

i. Sales commissions: _____

j. Salaries of distribution center personnel: _____

k. Wages of sewing machine operators: _____

l. Factory janitorial supplies: _____

m. Chief financial officer's salary: _____

n. Travel costs of media relations employees: _____

o. Factory supervisors' salaries: _____

p. Oil used to lubricate office equipment: _____

q. Property taxes on factory building and equipment: _____

EXERCISE 16-5

a. _____

b. _____

c. _____

d. _____

e. _____

f. _____

g. _____

EXERCISE 16-6

a. _____

b. _____

c. _____

d. _____

e. _____

f. _____

g. _____

EXERCISE 16-7

a. Cost to lease (rent) railroad cars: _____

b. Cost of track and bed (ballast) replacement: _____

c. Diesel fuel costs: _____

d. Cost to lease (rent) train locomotives: _____

e. Depreciation of terminal facilities: _____

f. Maintenance costs of right of way, bridges, and buildings: _____

g. Salaries of dispatching and communications personnel: _____

h. Headquarters information technology support staff salaries: _____

i. Safety training costs: _____

j. Wages of train engineers: _____

k. Wages of switch and classification yard personnel: _____

l. Costs of accident cleanup: _____

EXERCISE 16-8

1. _____

_____

_____

2. _____

_____

_____

_____

_____

_____

_____

Manufacturing Costs

EXERCISE 16-9

a.

Income Statement		

b. Inventory balances on January 31, 2016:

Materials: _____

_____

Work in Process: _____

_____

Finished Goods: _____

_____

EXERCISE 16-10

Balance Sheet

EXERCISE 16-11

EXERCISE 16-12

Work in process inventory, August 1	$ 22,400	$ 50,400	(e) _____
Total manufacturing costs incurred during August	156,800	(c) _____	58,800
Total manufacturing costs	(a) _____	$294,000	$68,600
Work in process inventory, August 31	33,600	67,200	(f) _____
Cost of goods manufactured	(b) _____	(d) _____	$60,200

EXERCISE 16-13

EXERCISE 16-14

Finished goods inventory, June 1	$ 61,600	$ 46,200	(e) _____
Cost of goods manufactured	329,000	(c) _____	484,800
Cost of finished goods available for sale	(a) _____	$260,400	$540,000
Finished goods inventory, June 30	72,800	61,600	(f) _____
Cost of goods sold	(b) _____	(d) _____	$513,600

EXERCISE 16-15

a.

Statement of Cost of Goods Manufactured			

EXERCISE 16-15, Concluded

b.

EXERCISE 16-16

a., b., and c.

EXERCISE 16-17

a. through e.

EXERCISE 16-18

This Page Not Used.

PROBLEM 16-1 ___

Cost	Product Costs			Period Costs	
	Direct Materials Cost	Direct Labor Cost	Factory Overhead Cost	Selling Expense	Administrative Expense
a.					
b.					
c.					
d.					
e.					
f.					
g.					
h.					
i.					
j.					
k.					
l.					
m.					
n.					
o.					
p.					
q.					
r.					
s.					
t.					
u.					
v.					
w.					
x.					
y.					
z.					

14

This Page Not Used.

PROBLEM 16-2 ___

Cost	Product Costs			Period Costs	
	Direct Materials Cost	Direct Labor Cost	Factory Overhead Cost	Selling Expense	Administrative Expense
a.					
b.					
c.					
d.					
e.					
f.					
g.					
h.					
i.					
j.					
k.					
l.					
m.					
n.					
o.					
p.					
q.					
r.					
s.					
t.					
u.					
v.					
w.					
x.					

This Page Not Used.

PROBLEM 16-3 ___

1. _____

   _____

   _____

   _____

   _____

2.

Cost	Direct	Indirect
a.		
b.		
c.		
d.		
e.		
f.		
g.		
h.		
i.		
j.		
k.		
l.		
m.		
n.		
o.		
p.		
q.		
r.		
s.		
t.		
u.		
v.		
w.		

18

This Page Not Used.

PROBLEM 16-4 ___

1. _____ Company

    a. _____

    b. _____

    c. _____

    d. _____

    e. _____

    f. _____

   _____ Company

    a. _____

    b. _____

    c. _____

    d. _____

    e. _____

    f. _____

PROBLEM 16-4 ___, Continued

2.

Statement of Cost of Goods Manufactured				

PROBLEM 16-4 ___, Concluded

3.

	Income Statement		

This Page Not Used.

PROBLEM 16-5 ___

1.

Statement of Cost of Goods Manufactured			

PROBLEM 16-5 ___, Concluded

2.

Income Statement			

EXERCISE 17-1

a. _____

b. _____

c. _____

d. _____

e. _____

EXERCISE 17-2

a. Cost of goods sold:

b. Direct materials cost:

c. Direct labor cost:

EXERCISE 17-3

a.

RECEIVED			ISSUED			BALANCE			
Receiving Report Number	Quantity	Unit Price	Materials Requisition Number	Quantity	Amount	Date	Quantity	Unit Price	Amount
						May 1	285	$30.00	$8,550
40	130	$32.00				May 4	_____	_____	_____
							_____	_____	_____
			91	365	_____	May 10	_____	_____	_____
44	110	38.00				May 21	_____	_____	_____
							_____	_____	_____
			97	100	_____	May 27	_____	_____	_____

b. _____

_____

c.

JOURNAL   PAGE

	DATE		DESCRIPTION	POST. REF.	DEBIT	CREDIT	
1							1
2							2
3							3
4							4

d. _____

_____

_____

_____

_____

_____

_____

_____

EXERCISE 17-4

JOURNAL

PAGE

	DATE		DESCRIPTION	POST. REF.	DEBIT	CREDIT	
1							1
2							2
3							3
4							4

EXERCISE 17-5

a. and b.

JOURNAL

PAGE

	DATE		DESCRIPTION	POST. REF.	DEBIT	CREDIT	
1							1
2							2
3							3
4							4
5							5
6							6
7							7
8							8

c.

	Fabric	Polyester Filling	Lumber	Glue

EXERCISE 17-6

JOURNAL

PAGE

	DATE		DESCRIPTION	POST. REF.	DEBIT	CREDIT	
1							1
2							2
3							3
4							4

EXERCISE 17-7

a.

JOURNAL   PAGE

	DATE		DESCRIPTION	POST. REF.	DEBIT	CREDIT	
1							1
2							2
3							3
4							4

Supporting calculations:

_____

b. _____

_____

_____

_____

_____

EXERCISE 17-8

a. and b.

JOURNAL　　　　　　　　　　　　　　　PAGE

	DATE		DESCRIPTION	POST. REF.	DEBIT	CREDIT	
1							1
2							2
3							3
4							4
5							5
6							6
7							7
8							8
9							9
10							10

EXERCISE 17-9

a. Factory 1 overhead rate: _____

_____

b. Factory 2 overhead rate: _____

_____

c.

JOURNAL　　　　　　　　　　　　　　　PAGE

	DATE		DESCRIPTION	POST. REF.	DEBIT	CREDIT	
1							1
2							2
3							3
4							4
5							5
6							6
7							7
8							8
9							9

d. Balance of Factory 1 accounts as of September 30: _____

_____

Balance of Factory 2 accounts as of September 30: _____

_____

EXERCISE 17-10

EXERCISE 17-11

a. _____

EXERCISE 17-12

a.

JOURNAL

PAGE _____

	DATE		DESCRIPTION	POST. REF.	DEBIT	CREDIT	
1							1
2							2
3							3
4							4

b.

EXERCISE 17-13

a. through d.

JOURNAL

	DATE		DESCRIPTION	POST. REF.	DEBIT	CREDIT	
1							1
2							2
3							3
4							4
5							5
6							6
7							7
8							8
9							9
10							10
11							11
12							12
13							13
14							14
15							15
16							16
17							17
18							18
19							19
20							20
21							21
22							22
23							23
24							24

EXERCISE 17-14

a.

	Income Statement		

b. Materials inventory:

Work in process inventory:

Finished goods inventory:

EXERCISE 17-15

a.

Date	Job No.	Quantity	Product	Amount	Unit Cost
Jan. 2	1	520	TT	$16,120	_____
Jan. 15	22	1,610	SS	20,125	_____
Feb. 3	30	1,420	SS	25,560	_____
Mar. 7	41	670	TT	15,075	_____
Mar. 24	49	2,210	SLK	22,100	_____
May 19	58	2,550	SLK	31,875	_____
June 12	65	620	TT	10,540	_____
Aug. 18	78	3,110	SLK	48,205	_____
Sept. 2	82	1,210	SS	16,940	_____
Nov. 14	92	750	TT	8,250	_____
Dec. 12	98	2,700	SLK	52,650	_____

Unit Costs for TT

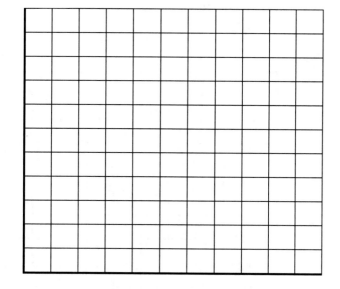

Job Number

EXERCISE 17-15, Continued

Unit Costs for SS

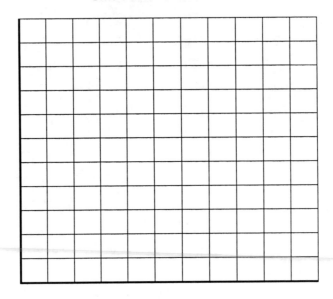

Job Number

Unit Costs for SLK

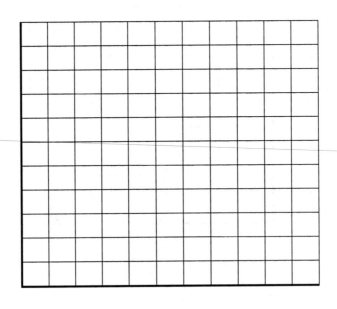

Job Number

_____

_____

_____

_____

EXERCISE 17-15, Concluded

b. _____

_____

_____

_____

_____

_____

_____

_____

_____

_____

_____

_____

_____

EXERCISE 17-16

a. _____

Job 101:

EXERCISE 17-16, Continued

Job 105:

EXERCISE 17-16, Concluded

b. _____

EXERCISE 17-17

a.

JOURNAL

PAGE

	DATE		DESCRIPTION	POST. REF.	DEBIT	CREDIT	
1							1
2							2
3							3
4							4
5							5
6							6
7							7
8							8
9							9
10							10
11							11
12							12
13							13
14							14
15							15
16							16
17							17
18							18
19							19
20							20
21							21
22							22
23							23
24							24
25							25
26							26
27							27
28							28
29							29
30							30
31							31
32							32
33							33
34							34
35							35

EXERCISE 17-17, Concluded

b.

c.

EXERCISE 17-18

a. through d.

JOURNAL   PAGE ____

	DATE		DESCRIPTION	POST. REF.	DEBIT	CREDIT	
1							1
2							2
3							3
4							4
5							5
6							6
7							7
8							8
9							9
10							10
11							11
12							12
13							13
14							14

Supporting calculations:

This Page Not Used.

PROBLEM 17-1 ___
a. through i.

JOURNAL

	DATE		DESCRIPTION	POST. REF.	DEBIT	CREDIT	
1							1
2							2
3							3
4							4
5							5
6							6
7							7
8							8
9							9
10							10
11							11
12							12
13							13
14							14
15							15
16							16
17							17
18							18
19							19
20							20
21							21
22							22
23							23
24							24
25							25
26							26
27							27
28							28
29							29
30							30
31							31
32							32
33							33
34							34
35							35

PROBLEM 17-1 ___, Concluded

JOURNAL   PAGE

	DATE		DESCRIPTION	POST. REF.	DEBIT	CREDIT	
1							1
2							2
3							3
4							4
5							5
6							6
7							7
8							8
9							9
10							10
11							11
12							12
13							13
14							14
15							15
16							16
17							17
18							18
19							19
20							20
21							21
22							22
23							23
24							24
25							25
26							26
27							27
28							28
29							29
30							30
31							31
32							32
33							33
34							34
35							35
36							36

PROBLEM 17-2 ___

1. a. through g.

	DATE		DESCRIPTION	POST. REF.	DEBIT	CREDIT	
1							1
2							2
3							3
4							4
5							5
6							6
7							7
8							8
9							9
10							10
11							11
12							12
13							13
14							14
15							15
16							16
17							17
18							18
19							19
20							20
21							21
22							22
23							23
24							24
25							25
26							26
27							27
28							28
29							29
30							30
31							31
32							32
33							33
34							34
35							35

JOURNAL PAGE

PROBLEM 17-2 ___ , Continued

f. Computation of cost of jobs finished:

g. Computation of cost of jobs sold:

2.

Work in Process

Finished Goods

PROBLEM 17-2 ___, Concluded

3.

Schedule of Unfinished Jobs

JOB	DIRECT MATERIALS	DIRECT LABOR	FACTORY OVERHEAD	TOTAL

4.

Schedule of Completed Jobs

JOB	DIRECT MATERIALS	DIRECT LABOR	FACTORY OVERHEAD	TOTAL

This Page Not Used.

PROBLEM 17-3 ___

1. and 2.

JOB ORDER COST SHEET

Customer _____   Date   _____
                                             Date wanted   _____
                                             Date completed _____
                                             Job No.   _____

ESTIMATE

Direct Materials		Amount	Direct Labor		Amount	Summary	Amount
____ meters at $_____		_____	____ hours at $_____		_____	Direct materials	_____
____ meters at ____		_____	____ hours at ____		_____	Direct labor	_____
____ meters at ____		_____	____ hours at ____		_____	Factory overhead	_____
____ meters at ____		_____	____ hours at ____		_____		
Total		_____	Total		_____	Total cost	_____

ACTUAL

Mat. Req. No.	Description	Amount	Time Ticket No.	Description	Amount	Item	Amount
____	_____	_____	____	_____	_____	Direct materials	_____
____	_____	_____	____	_____	_____	Direct labor	_____
____	_____	_____	____	_____	_____	Factory overhead	_____
____							
Total		_____	Total		_____	Total cost	_____

Comments:

This Page Not Used.

PROBLEM 17-4 ___

1. Supporting calculations:

Job No.	Quantity	Work in Process Direct Materials	Work in Process Direct Labor	Work in Process Factory Overhead	Total Cost	Unit Cost	Units Sold	Cost of Goods Sold

(A)

(B)

(C)

(D)

(E)

(F)

(G)

(H)

PROBLEM 17-4 ___, Concluded

2. _____

_____

_____

_____

_____

_____

_____

_____

_____

_____

_____

_____

_____

_____

_____

_____

_____

_____

_____

PROBLEM 17-5 ___

1.

Income Statement			

Supporting calculations:

PROBLEM 17-5 ___, Concluded

2. _____

_____

_____

_____

_____

_____

_____

_____

_____

_____

_____

_____

EXERCISE 18-1

a. through e.

JOURNAL   PAGE _____

	DATE		DESCRIPTION	POST. REF.	DEBIT	CREDIT	
1							1
2							2
3							3
4							4
5							5
6							6
7							7
8							8
9							9
10							10
11							11
12							12
13							13
14							14
15							15
16							16
17							17
18							18
19							19
20							20
21							21
22							22
23							23
24							24
25							25

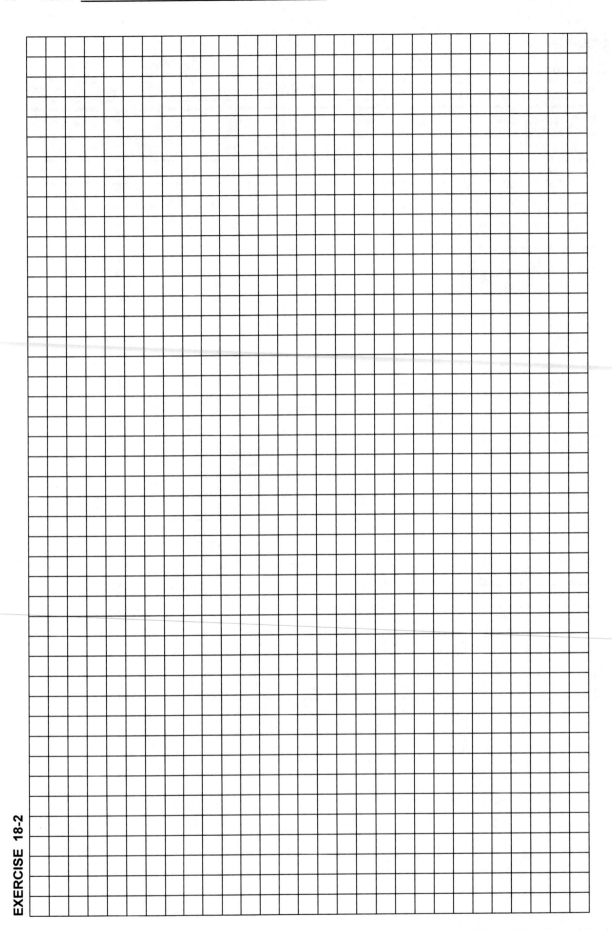

EXERCISE 18-3

a. and b.

JOURNAL

	DATE		DESCRIPTION	POST. REF.	DEBIT	CREDIT	
1							1
2							2
3							3
4							4
5							5
6							6
7							7
8							8
9							9
10							10
11							11
12							12
13							13
14							14
15							15
16							16
17							17
18							18
19							19
20							20

EXERCISE 18-4

a. _____

_____

b.

JOURNAL   PAGE

	DATE		DESCRIPTION	POST. REF.	DEBIT	CREDIT	
1							1
2							2
3							3
4							4
5							5
6							6
7							7

c. _____

d. _____

EXERCISE 18-5

	A	B	C	D
1			**Equivalent Units**	
2		**Whole Units**	**Direct Materials**	**Conversion**
3				
4				
5				
6				
7				
8				
9				
10				
11				
12				

EXERCISE 18-6

a. Drawing Department

	A	B	C	D
1			**Equivalent Units**	
2		**Whole Units**	**Direct Materials**	**Conversion**
3				
4				
5				
6				
7				
8				
9				
10				
11				
12				
13				
14				
15				
16				

b. Winding Department

	A	B	C	D
1			**Equivalent Units**	
2		**Whole Units**	**Direct Materials**	**Conversion**
3				
4				
5				
6				
7				
8				
9				
10				
11				
12				
13				
14				
15				
16				

EXERCISE 18-7

a.

EXERCISE 18-7, Concluded

b.

	A	B	C	D
			Equivalent Units	
		Whole Units	Direct Materials	Conversion
1				
2				
3				
4				
5				
6				
7				
8				
9				
10				
11				
12				
13				
14				
15				
16				

EXERCISE 18-8

a. 1. _____

2. _____

3. _____

4. _____

5. _____

EXERCISE 18-8, Concluded

b. _____

_____

EXERCISE 18-9

Equivalent units of production:

	CEREAL (IN POUNDS)	BOXES (IN BOXES)	CONVERSION COST (IN BOXES)

Supporting explanation:

_____

_____

_____

_____

_____

_____

_____

_____

_____

_____

_____

_____

_____

_____

_____

_____

_____

_____

_____

_____

_____

_____

EXERCISE 18-10

a.

b.

c.

EXERCISE 18-11

a.

b.

	A	B	C	D
1			Equivalent Units	
2		Whole Units	Direct Materials	Conversion
3				
4				
5				
6				
7				
8				
9				
10				
11				
12				
13				
14				

c.

	A	B	C
1		Costs	
2		Direct Materials	Conversion
3			
4			
5			
6			
7			
8			
9			
10			

d. _____

EXERCISE 18-12

a. 1. _____

2. _____

3. _____

4. _____

b. _____

_____

_____

_____

_____

_____

_____

_____

_____

EXERCISE 18-12, Concluded

c. _____

_____

EXERCISE 18-13

EXERCISE 18-14

a. _____

b.

	A	B	C	D
			Equivalent Units	
1		Whole Units	Direct Materials	Conversion
2				
3				
4				
5				
6				
7				
8				
9				
10				
11				
12				
13				
14				
15				

	A	B	C
		Costs	
1		Direct Materials	Conversion
2			
3			
4			
5			
6			
7			
8			
9			
10			

c. _____

EXERCISE 18-15

a. _____

b. _____

c. _____

d. _____

_____

e. _____

_____

_____

EXERCISE 18-16

a. 1. through 4.

	A	B	C	D
1				
2	Cost of Production Report—_____			
3				
4			Equivalent Units	
5	UNITS	Whole Units	Direct Materials	Conversion
6				
7				
8				
9				
10				
11				
12				
13				
14				
15				
16				
17				
18				
19				
20				
21				
22				
23				
24				
25				
26				
27				
28				
29				
30				

EXERCISE 18-16, Continued

	A	B	C	D
			Costs	
1				
2	COSTS	Direct Materials	Conversion	Total
3				
4				
5				
6				
7				
8				
9				
10				
11				
12				
13				
14				
15				
16				
17				
18				
19				
20				
21				
22				
23				
24				
25				
26				
27				
28				
29				
30				
31				
32				
33				
34				
35				
36				
37				
38				
39				
40				
41				
42				

EXERCISE 18-16, Concluded

b.

EXERCISE 18-17

a.

	A	B	C	D
1				
2	Cost of Production Report—_____			
3				
4			Equivalent Units	
5	UNITS	Whole Units	Direct Materials	Conversion
6				
7				
8				
9				
10				
11				
12				
13				
14				
15				
16				
17				
18				
19				
20				
21				
22				
23				
24				
25				
26				
27				
28				
29				
30				

EXERCISE 18-17, Continued

	A	B	C	D
1			Costs	
2	COSTS	Direct Materials	Conversion	Total
3				
4				
5				
6				
7				
8				
9				
10				
11				
12				
13				
14				
15				
16				
17				
18				
19				
20				
21				
22				
23				
24				
25				
26				
27				
28				
29				
30				
31				
32				
33				
34				
35				
36				
37				
38				
39				
40				
41				
42				

EXERCISE 18-17, Concluded

b.

EXERCISE 18-18

a. 1. through 3.

JOURNAL   PAGE

	DATE		DESCRIPTION	POST. REF.	DEBIT	CREDIT	
1							1
2							2
3							3
4							4
5							5
6							6
7							7
8							8
9							9
10							10
11							11
12							12
13							13
14							14
15							15

EXERCISE 18-18, Continued

Supporting calculations:

	A	B	C	D
			Equivalent Units	
1		**Whole Units**	**Direct Materials**	**Conversion**
2				
3				
4				
5				
6				
7				
8				
9				
10				
11				
12				
13				
14				
15				
16				
17				
18				

EXERCISE 18-18, Concluded

b. _____

c.

EXERCISE 18-19

a. 1. through 3.

JOURNAL

	DATE		DESCRIPTION	POST. REF.	DEBIT	CREDIT	
1							1
2							2
3							3
4							4
5							5
6							6
7							7
8							8
9							9
10							10
11							11
12							12
13							13
14							14
15							15

EXERCISE 18-19, Continued

Supporting calculations:

	A	B	C	D
1			Equivalent Units	
2		Whole Units	Direct Materials	Conversion
3				
4				
5				
6				
7				
8				
9				
10				
11				
12				
13				
14				
15				

EXERCISE 18-19, Concluded

b. _____

EXERCISE 18-20

a. Cost per megawatt hour (MWh) for the fossil fuel plant:

_____

_____

_____

Cost per megawatt hour (MWh) for the wind farm:

_____

_____

_____

Lowest cost facility:

_____

_____

_____

EXERCISE 18-20, Concluded

b. _____

_____

_____

_____

_____

_____

_____

_____

_____

_____

_____

c. _____

_____

_____

_____

_____

_____

_____

_____

_____

_____

EXERCISE 18-21

_____
_____
_____
_____
_____

	A	B	C	D	E
1					
2					
3					
4					
5					

_____
_____
_____
_____
_____
_____
_____
_____
_____

	A	B	C	D	E
1					
2					
3					
4					
5					
6					
7					
8					
9					
10					
11					
12					

EXERCISE 18-21, Concluded

EXERCISE 18-22

a.

	A	B	C	D	E	F	G
1		January	February	March	April	May	June
2							
3							
4							
5							

_____

_____

_____

_____

_____

EXERCISE 18-22, Concluded

b. _____

_____

_____

_____

_____

_____

_____

_____

_____

_____

_____

_____

_____

_____

_____

_____

_____

_____

_____

_____

_____

_____

_____

_____

_____

_____

_____

_____

_____

_____

_____

_____

_____

EXERCISE 18-23

_____

_____

_____

_____

_____

_____

_____

_____

_____

_____

_____

_____

_____

_____

_____

_____

_____

_____

_____

_____

_____

_____

_____

_____

_____

_____

_____

_____

_____

_____

_____

_____

_____

_____

EXERCISE 18-23, Concluded

APPENDIX EXERCISE 18-24

a. and b.

	A	B	C
1		a. Whole Units	b. Equivalent Units of Production
2			
3			
4			
5			
6			
7			
8			
9			
10			
11			
12			
13			
14			
15			

APPENDIX EXERCISE 18-25

a. Drawing Department

	A	B	C
1		Whole Units	Equivalent Units of Production
2			
3			
4			
5			
6			
7			
8			
9			
10			
11			
12			
13			
14			
15			

APPENDIX EXERCISE 18-25, Concluded

b. Winding Department

	A	B	C
1		**Whole Units**	**Equivalent Units of Production**
2			
3			
4			
5			
6			
7			
8			
9			
10			
11			
12			
13			
14			
15			

APPENDIX EXERCISE 18-26

a.

b.

	A	B	C
1		**Whole Units**	**Equivalent Units of Production**
2			
3			
4			
5			
6			
7			
8			
9			
10			
11			
12			
13			
14			
15			

APPENDIX EXERCISE 18-27

a. and b.

	A	B Whole Units	C Equivalent Units of Production
1			
2			
3			
4			
5			
6			
7			
8			
9			
10			
11			
12			
13			
14			
15			

c. _____

d. _____

e. _____

APPENDIX EXERCISE 18-28

a.

	A	B	C
		Whole Units	**Equivalent Units of Production**
1			
2			
3			
4			
5			
6			
7			
8			
9			
10			
11			
12			
13			
14			
15			

_____

_____

_____

_____

_____

_____

_____

b. _____

_____

c. _____

_____

APPENDIX EXERCISE 18-29

	A	B	C
1			
2	Cost of Production Report—_____		
3			
4	UNITS	Whole Units	Equivalent Units of Production
5			
6			
7			
8			
9			
10			
11			
12			
13			
14			
15			
16			
17			
18			
19			
20			

	A	B
1	COSTS	Costs
2		
3		
4		
5		
6		
7		
8		
9		
10		
11		
12		
13		
14		
15		
16		
17		
18		
19		
20		
21		
22		

APPENDIX EXERCISE 18-30

	A	B	C
1			
2	Cost of Production Report—_____		
3			
4	UNITS	Whole Units	Equivalent Units of Production
5			
6			
7			
8			
9			
10			
11			
12			
13			
14			
15			
16			
17			
18			

	A	B
1	COSTS	Costs
2		
3		
4		
5		
6		
7		
8		
9		
10		
11		
12		
13		
14		
15		
16		
17		
18		
19		
20		
21		
22		
23		
24		

PROBLEM 18-1 ___

1. a. through i.

JOURNAL   PAGE

	DATE		DESCRIPTION	POST. REF.	DEBIT	CREDIT	
1							1
2							2
3							3
4							4
5							5
6							6
7							7
8							8
9							9
10							10
11							11
12							12
13							13
14							14
15							15
16							16
17							17
18							18
19							19
20							20
21							21
22							22
23							23
24							24
25							25
26							26
27							27
28							28
29							29
30							30
31							31
32							32
33							33
34							34
35							35

PROBLEM 18-1 ___ , Continued

JOURNAL

	DATE	DESCRIPTION	POST. REF.	DEBIT	CREDIT	
1						1
2						2
3						3
4						4
5						5
6						6
7						7
8						8
9						9
10						10
11						11
12						12
13						13
14						14
15						15
16						16
17						17
18						18
19						19
20						20
21						21
22						22
23						23
24						24
25						25
26						26
27						27
28						28
29						29
30						30
31						31
32						32
33						33
34						34
35						35
36						36

PROBLEM 18-1 ____, Concluded

2.

	MATERIALS	WORK IN PROCESS— _____ DEPT.	WORK IN PROCESS— _____ DEPT.	FINISHED GOODS

3.

	FACTORY OVERHEAD— _____ DEPT.	FACTORY OVERHEAD— _____ DEPT.

100

This Page Not Used.

PROBLEM 18-2 ___

1.

	A	B	C	D
1				
2	Cost of Production Report—_____			
3				
4			Equivalent Units	
5	UNITS	Whole Units	Direct Materials	Conversion
6				
7				
8				
9				
10				
11				
12				
13				
14				
15				
16				
17				
18				
19				
20				
21				
22				
23				
24				
25				
26				
27				
28				
29				
30				
31				
32				
33				
34				
35				
36				
37				
38				
39				
40				
41				
42				

PROBLEM 18-2 ___, Continued

	Costs		
COSTS	Direct Materials	Conversion	Total

PROBLEM 18-2 ___, Concluded

2. _____

_____

_____

_____

_____

_____

_____

_____

_____

_____

_____

Computations:

This Page Not Used.

PROBLEM 18-3 ___

1.

	A	B	C	D
1				
2	Cost of Production Report—_____			
3				
4			Equivalent Units	
5	UNITS	Whole Units	Direct Materials	Conversion
6				
7				
8				
9				
10				
11				
12				
13				
14				
15				
16				
17				
18				
19				
20				
21				
22				
23				
24				
25				
26				
27				
28				
29				
30				
31				
32				
33				
34				
35				
36				
37				
38				
39				
40				
41				
42				

PROBLEM 18-3 ___, Continued

	A	B	C	D
		Costs		
	COSTS	Direct Materials	Conversion	Total
3				
4				
5				
6				
7				
8				
9				
10				
11				
12				
13				
14				
15				
16				
17				
18				
19				
20				
21				
22				
23				
24				
25				
26				
27				
28				
29				
30				
31				
32				
33				
34				
35				
36				
37				
38				
39				
40				
41				
42				

PROBLEM 18-3 ___, Concluded

2.

JOURNAL   PAGE

	DATE		DESCRIPTION	POST. REF.	DEBIT	CREDIT	
1							1
2							2
3							3
4							4
5							5
6							6
7							7
8							8
9							9
10							10

3. _____

_____

4. _____

_____

_____

_____

_____

_____

_____

_____

_____

_____

_____

_____

_____

_____

This Page Not Used.

PROBLEM 18-4 ___

1. and 2.

ACCOUNT   *Work in Process—_____ Department*   ACCOUNT NO.

DATE		ITEM	DEBIT	CREDIT	BALANCE	
					DEBIT	CREDIT

PROBLEM 18-4 ___, Continued

1.

	A	B	C	D
	Cost of Production Report—_____			
			Equivalent Units	
			Direct Materials (a)	**Conversion (a)**
	UNITS	**Whole Units**		
6				
7				
8				
9				
10				
11				
12				
13				
14				
15				
16				
17				
18				
19				
20				
21				
22				
23				
24				
25				
26				
27				
28				
29				
30				
31				
32				
33				
34				
35				
36				
37				
38				
39				
40				
41				
42				

PROBLEM 18-4 ___, Continued

	A	B	C	D
			Costs	
	COSTS	Direct Materials	Conversion	Total
3				
4				
5				
6				
7				
8				
9				
10				
11				
12				
13				
14				
15				
16				
17				
18				
19				
20				
21				
22				
23				
24				
25				
26				
27				
28				
29				
30				
31				
32				
33				
34				
35				
36				
37				
38				
39				
40				
41				
42				

PROBLEM 18-4 ___, Continued

2.

	A	B	C	D
1				
2	Cost of Production Report—_____			
3				
4			Equivalent Units	
5	UNITS	Whole Units	Direct Materials (a)	Conversion (a)
6				
7				
8				
9				
10				
11				
12				
13				
14				
15				
16				
17				
18				
19				
20				
21				
22				
23				
24				
25				
26				
27				
28				
29				
30				
31				
32				
33				
34				
35				
36				
37				
38				
39				
40				
41				
42				

PROBLEM 18-4 ___ , Continued

	A	B	C	D
1			Costs	
2	COSTS	Direct Materials	Conversion	Total
3				
4				
5				
6				
7				
8				
9				
10				
11				
12				
13				
14				
15				
16				
17				
18				
19				
20				
21				
22				
23				
24				
25				
26				
27				
28				
29				
30				
31				
32				
33				
34				
35				
36				
37				
38				
39				
40				
41				
42				

PROBLEM 18-4 ___ , Concluded

3. _____

_____

_____

_____

_____

_____

_____

_____

APPENDIX PROBLEM 18-5 ___

	A	B	C
1			
2	Cost of Production Report—_____		
3			
4	UNITS	Whole Units	Equivalent Units of Production
5			
6			
7			
8			
9			
10			
11			
12			
13			
14			
15			
16			
17			
18			
19			
20			
21			
22			
23			
24			
25			
26			
27			
28			
29			
30			
31			
32			
33			
34			
35			
36			
37			
38			
39			
40			
41			
42			

APPENDIX PROBLEM 18-5 ___, Concluded

	A	B
1	COSTS	Costs
2		
3		
4		
5		
6		
7		
8		
9		
10		
11		
12		
13		
14		
15		
16		
17		
18		
19		
20		
21		
22		
23		
24		
25		
26		
27		
28		
29		
30		
31		
32		
33		
34		
35		
36		
37		
38		
39		
40		
41		
42		

EXERCISE 19-1

1. _____   9. _____

2. _____   10. _____

3. _____   11. _____

4. _____   12. _____

5. _____   13. _____

6. _____   14. _____

7. _____   15. _____

8. _____

EXERCISE 19-2

a. _____   d. _____

b. _____   e. _____

c. _____

EXERCISE 19-3

1. Financial aid office salaries: _____

2. Office supplies: _____

3. Instructor salaries: _____

4. Housing personnel wages: _____

5. Student records office salaries: _____

6. Admissions office salaries: _____

EXERCISE 19-4

1. Preparation costs for each car received: _____

2. Salespersons' commission of 5% of the sales price for each car sold: _____

3. Administrative costs for ordering cars: _____

EXERCISE 19-5

a. _____   g. _____

b. _____   h. _____

c. _____   i. _____

d. _____   j. _____

e. _____   k. _____

f. _____

EXERCISE 19-6

Components produced	200,000		400,000		600,000
Total costs:					
Total variable costs	$250,000	(d) _____		(j) _____	
Total fixed costs	600,000	(e) _____		(k) _____	
Total costs	$850,000	(f) _____		(l) _____	
Cost per unit:					
Variable cost per unit	(a) _____	(g) _____		(m) _____	
Fixed cost per unit	(b) _____	(h) _____		(n) _____	
Total cost per unit	(c) _____	(i) _____		(o) _____	

Supporting calculations:

_____

_____

_____

_____

_____

_____

_____

_____

_____

_____

_____

_____

_____

_____

_____

_____

_____

_____

_____

_____

_____

_____

_____

_____

EXERCISE 19-7

a. Variable Cost per Unit: _____

_____

_____

_____

_____

_____

_____

_____

Fixed Cost: _____

_____

_____

_____

_____

_____

_____

_____

_____

_____

_____

_____

_____

_____

_____

b. _____

_____

EXERCISE 19-8

Variable Cost per Gross-Ton Mile: _____

_____

_____

_____

_____

_____

_____

_____

_____

_____

_____

Fixed Cost: _____

_____

_____

_____

_____

_____

_____

_____

_____

_____

_____

_____

_____

_____

_____

_____

EXERCISE 19-9

a.

b.

EXERCISE 19-10

a.

b.

EXERCISE 19-10, Concluded

c.

EXERCISE 19-11

a. _____

_____

_____

_____

_____

b. _____

_____

_____

_____

_____

_____

_____

EXERCISE 19-12

a. _____

_____

_____

_____

_____

_____

EXERCISE 19-12, Concluded

b. _____

_____

_____

_____

_____

Calculations:

EXERCISE 19-13

a. _____

_____

_____

_____

_____

b. _____

_____

_____

_____

_____

EXERCISE 19-14

_____

_____

_____

_____

_____

_____

_____

_____

_____

_____

_____

_____

_____

_____

_____

EXERCISE 19-15

EXERCISE 19-16

a. _____

_____

_____

_____

_____

_____

_____

Calculations:

_____

_____

EXERCISE 19-16, Concluded

b. _____

_____

_____

_____

_____

_____

_____

_____

_____

_____

_____

_____

_____

_____

_____

_____

_____

EXERCISE 19-17

a.

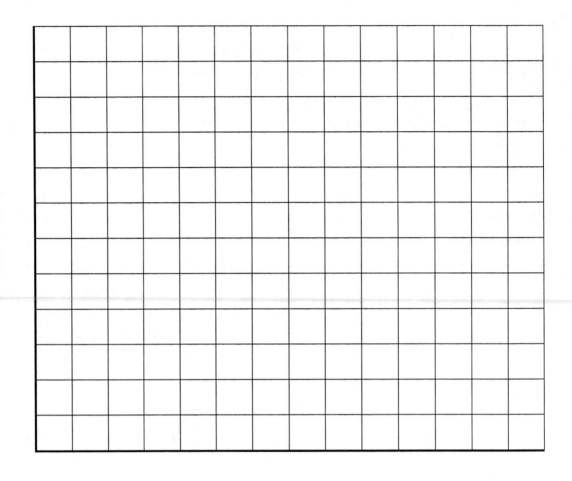

b. _____
_____

c. _____
_____
_____
_____
_____

EXERCISE 19-18

a. _____
   _____

b.

c.

Operating Profit (Loss)

Units of Sales

d. _____
   _____

EXERCISE 19-19

Chart name: _____

a. _____

b. _____

c. _____

d. _____

e. _____

f. _____

EXERCISE 19-20

Chart name: _____

a. _____

b. _____

c. _____

d. _____

e. _____

f. _____

EXERCISE 19-21

a. _____

_____

_____

_____

_____

_____

_____

_____

_____

_____

_____

_____

_____

_____

b. Baseball bats: _____

_____

Baseball gloves: _____

_____

EXERCISE 19-22

a. _____

_____

_____

_____

_____

_____

_____

Supporting calculations:

b.

EXERCISE 19-23

a. (1) In dollars: _____

_____

_____

_____

_____

(2) As a percentage of sales: _____

_____

_____

_____

_____

b. _____

_____

_____

_____

_____

_____

_____

_____

_____

_____

_____

_____

_____

_____

_____

_____

_____

_____

_____

_____

EXERCISE 19-24

_____

_____

_____

EXERCISE 19-25

a. Beck Inc.: _____

_____

_____

_____

_____

_____

Bryant Inc.: _____

_____

_____

_____

_____

_____

_____

b. _____

_____

_____

_____

_____

c. _____

_____

_____

_____

_____

_____

_____

APPENDIX EXERCISE 19-26

a. _____

b. _____

c. _____

APPENDIX EXERCISE 19-27

a.

Income Statement—Variable Costing		

Computations:

_____

_____

_____

_____

_____

_____

_____

_____

_____

_____

_____

_____

_____

_____

_____

_____

APPENDIX EXERCISE 19-27, Concluded

b.

APPENDIX EXERCISE 19-28

a.

Income Statement—Absorption Costing		

Computations:

_____

_____

_____

_____

_____

_____

b.

PROBLEM 19-1 ___

Cost	Fixed Cost	Variable Cost	Mixed Cost
a.			
b.			
c.			
d.			
e.			
f.			
g.			
h.			
i.			
j.			
k.			
l.			
m.			
n.			
o.			
p.			
q.			
r.			
s.			
t.			

This Page Not Used.

PROBLEM 19-2 ___

1.

2.

   a. Unit variable cost: _____

_____

   b. Unit contribution margin: _____

_____

3. _____

_____

_____

_____

_____

_____

_____

PROBLEM 19-2 ___, Continued

4. _____

5. _____

6.

7.

PROBLEM 19-2 ___, Concluded

8. _____

_____

_____

_____

_____

_____

_____

_____

_____

_____

_____

_____

_____

_____

_____

_____

_____

_____

_____

_____

_____

_____

_____

_____

_____

_____

_____

_____

_____

142

This Page Not Used.

© 2016 Cengage Learning. All Rights Reserved. May not be scanned, copied or duplicated, or posted to a publicly accessible website, in whole or in part.

PROBLEM 19-3 ___

1. _____

_____

_____

_____

_____

_____

_____

_____

_____

_____

_____

_____

_____

_____

2. _____

_____

_____

_____

_____

_____

_____

_____

_____

_____

_____

_____

_____

_____

PROBLEM 19-3 ___, Concluded

3.

Sales and Costs

Units of Sales

4.

PROBLEM 19-4 ___

1.

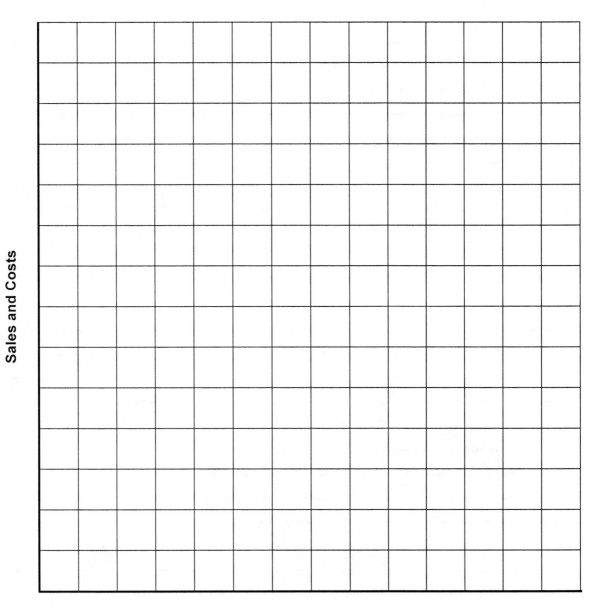

Sales and Costs

Units of Sales

PROBLEM 19-4 ___, Continued

_____

_____

_____

_____

_____

_____

_____

_____

_____

_____

_____

_____

_____

_____

_____

_____

_____

_____

_____

_____

_____

_____

_____

_____

_____

_____

_____

_____

_____

_____

_____

_____

_____

_____

_____

_____

_____

_____

PROBLEM 19-4 ___, Continued

2.

Sales and Costs

Units of Sales

PROBLEM 19-4 ___, Continued

3.

Sales and Costs

Units of Sales

PROBLEM 19-4 ___ , Continued

_____

_____

_____

_____

_____

_____

_____

_____

_____

_____

_____

_____

_____

_____

_____

_____

_____

_____

_____

_____

_____

_____

_____

_____

_____

_____

_____

_____

_____

_____

_____

_____

_____

_____

_____

_____

_____

_____

_____

_____

_____

PROBLEM 19-4 ___, Concluded

4.

Sales and Costs

Units of Sales

PROBLEM 19-5 ___

1.

_____

_____

_____

_____

_____

_____

_____

_____

_____

_____

2. _____

_____

_____

_____

_____

PROBLEM 19-5 ___, Concluded

3.

PROBLEM 19-6 ___

1.

	Estimated Income Statement			

PROBLEM 19-6 ___, Continued

2. _____

_____

_____

_____

_____

_____

_____

_____

_____

_____

3. _____

_____

_____

_____

_____

_____

_____

_____

_____

_____

_____

_____

_____

_____

_____

_____

_____

PROBLEM 19-6 ___, Continued

4.

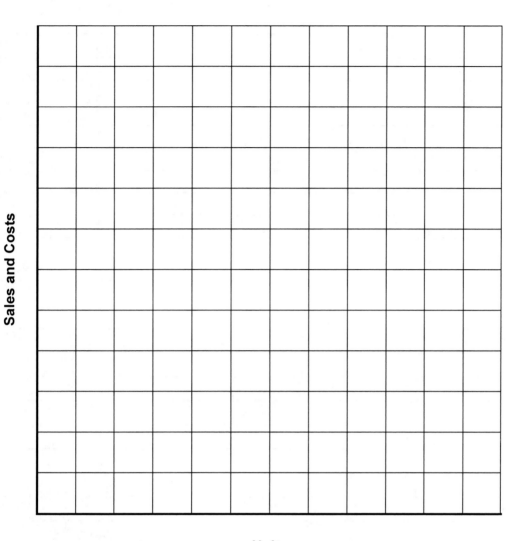

PROBLEM 19-6 ___, Concluded

5.

6.

EXERCISE 20-1

a. Under the absorption costing concept: _____

_____

_____

_____

_____

b. Under the variable costing concept: _____

_____

_____

_____

_____

EXERCISE 20-2

a.

Absorption Costing Income Statement

Supporting calculations:

EXERCISE 20-2, Continued

b.

Variable Costing Income Statement		

EXERCISE 20-2, Concluded

c. _____

_____

_____

_____

_____

_____

_____

_____

_____

_____

_____

_____

_____

_____

_____

_____

_____

_____

_____

_____

_____

EXERCISE 20-3

a.

Absorption Costing Income Statement		

b.

Variable Costing Income Statement		

EXERCISE 20-3, Concluded

c. _____

_____

_____

_____

_____

_____

_____

_____

_____

_____

_____

_____

_____

_____

_____

_____

_____

_____

_____

_____

_____

_____

_____

EXERCISE 20-4

a. Variable cost of goods manufactured per unit: _____

_____

_____

_____

_____

_____

_____

EXERCISE 20-4, Concluded

b. Absorption cost of goods manufactured per unit: _____

_____

_____

_____

_____

_____

_____

_____

_____

_____

_____

EXERCISE 20-5

Variable Costing Income Statement		

EXERCISE 20-6

Absorption Costing Income Statement		

EXERCISE 20-7

a.

Variable Costing Income Statement (assumed)		
(in millions)		

b. _____

_____

_____

_____

_____

_____

_____

_____

EXERCISE 20-8

a. (1)

Absorption Costing Income Statement		
	28,800 UNITS MANUFACTURED	36,000 UNITS MANUFACTURED

Supporting calculations:

EXERCISE 20-8, Continued

(2)

	Variable Costing Income Statement	

	28,800 UNITS MANUFACTURED	36,000 UNITS MANUFACTURED

Supporting calculations:

EXERCISE 20-8, Concluded

b. _____

_____

_____

_____

_____

_____

_____

_____

_____

_____

_____

_____

_____

_____

_____

_____

_____

_____

EXERCISE 20-9

a.

Variable Costing Income Statement (assumed)		
(in millions)		

Supporting calculations:

EXERCISE 20-9, Concluded

b. _____

_____

_____

_____

_____

_____

_____

_____

_____

_____

_____

_____

_____

_____

_____

_____

_____

_____

_____

_____

_____

_____

_____

_____

_____

_____

_____

EXERCISE 20-10

a. _____

_____

_____

_____

_____

_____

_____

_____

_____

_____

_____

_____

b.

Variable Costing Income Statements—Three Product Lines

	CROSS TRAINING SHOES	GOLF SHOES	RUNNING SHOES	

EXERCISE 20-10, Concluded

c. _____

_____

_____

_____

_____

_____

_____

_____

_____

_____

_____

_____

EXERCISE 20-11

_____

_____

_____

_____

_____

_____

_____

_____

EXERCISE 20-12

a.

Contribution Margin by Product		
	MOUNTAIN MONSTER	DESERT DRAGON

b. _____

_____

_____

_____

_____

_____

EXERCISE 20-13

a.

Contribution Margin by Territory		
	EAST COAST	WEST COAST

EXERCISE 20-13, Concluded

b. _____

_____

_____

_____

_____

_____

_____

_____

_____

_____

_____

_____

_____

_____

_____

_____

_____

_____

_____

_____

_____

_____

_____

_____

_____

_____

_____

EXERCISE 20-14

a. 1.

	CASSY G.	TODD	TIM	JEFF	
Contribution Margin by Salesperson					

2. _____

_____

_____

_____

_____

_____

_____

_____

_____

_____

_____

_____

_____

_____

_____

_____

_____

_____

_____

_____

EXERCISE 20-14, Concluded

b. 1.

Contribution Margin by Territory		
	NORTHEAST	SOUTHWEST

2. _____

_____

_____

_____

_____

_____

_____

_____

_____

_____

_____

_____

_____

_____

_____

_____

EXERCISE 20-15

a.

Contribution Margin by Segment (assumed)

(in millions, except ratio figures)

	BUILDING CONSTRUCTION PRODUCTS	CAT JAPAN	CORE COMPONENTS	EARTHMOVING	ELECTRIC POWER	EXCAVATION	LARGE POWER SYSTEMS	LOGISTICS	MARINE & PETROLEUM POWER	MINING	TURBINES

EXERCISE 20-15, Continued

b.

	BUILDING CONSTRUCTION PRODUCTS	CAT JAPAN	CORE COMPONENTS	EARTHMOVING	ELECTRIC POWER	EXCAVATION	LARGE POWER SYSTEMS	LOGISTICS	MARINE & PETROLEUM POWER	MINING	TURBINES

EXERCISE 20-15, Concluded

c. _____

_____

_____

_____

_____

_____

_____

_____

_____

_____

_____

_____

_____

_____

_____

_____

_____

_____

_____

_____

_____

_____

_____

_____

EXERCISE 20-16

a.

		FILMED ENTERTAINMENT	NETWORKS	PUBLISHING	
Contribution Margin by Segment (assumed)					
(in millions, except ratio figures)					

EXERCISE 20-16, Continued

b. _____

EXERCISE 20-16, Concluded

c. _____

_____

_____

_____

_____

_____

_____

_____

_____

_____

_____

_____

_____

_____

_____

_____

EXERCISE 20-17

a.

Contribution Margin Analysis—Sales		

b. _____

_____

_____

_____

_____

_____

_____

_____

_____

EXERCISE 20-18

Contribution Margin Analysis—Sales		

EXERCISE 20-19

Contribution Margin Analysis—Variable Costs		

EXERCISE 20-20

a.

		Contribution Margin by Route		

	ATLANTA/ BALTIMORE	BALTIMORE/ PITTSBURGH	PITTSBURGH/ ATLANTA	TOTAL

EXERCISE 20-20, Concluded

b. _____

_____

_____

_____

_____

_____

_____

_____

_____

_____

_____

_____

_____

_____

_____

_____

_____

EXERCISE 20-21

a.

Contribution Margin Report for Atlanta/Baltimore Route		

EXERCISE 20-21, Concluded

b.

Contribution Margin Analysis—Atlanta/Baltimore Route		

EXERCISE 20-22

a.

	Variable Costing Income Statement		

Supporting calculations:

_____

_____

_____

_____

_____

EXERCISE 20-22, Concluded

b.

Contribution Margin Analysis			

This Page Not Used.

PROBLEM 20-1 ___

1.

	Absorption Costing Income Statement		

PROBLEM 20-1 ___ , Concluded

2.

	Variable Costing Income Statement		

3. _____

_____

_____

_____

_____

_____

_____

_____

_____

_____

_____

PROBLEM 20-2 ___

1.

*Estimated Income Statement—Absorption Costing—*_____		

PROBLEM 20-1 ___ , Concluded

2.

	Estimated Income Statement—Variable Costing— _____		

3. _____

4. _____

PROBLEM 20-3 ___

1. a.

Absorption Costing Income Statement		

b.

Absorption Costing Income Statement		

PROBLEM 20-3 ___, Continued

2. a.

Variable Costing Income Statement		

PROBLEM 20-3 ___, Continued

b.

Variable Costing Income Statement		

PROBLEM 20-3 ___, Concluded

3. a. _____

_____

_____

_____

_____

_____

_____

_____

_____

_____

_____

_____

b. _____

_____

_____

_____

_____

_____

_____

_____

_____

_____

_____

_____

4. _____

_____

_____

_____

_____

_____

_____

_____

_____

PROBLEM 20-4 ___

1.

Salesperson	Contribution Margin	Variable Cost of Goods Sold as a Percent of Sales	Variable Selling Expenses as a Percent of Sales	Contribution Margin Ratio

Salespersons' Analysis

For the Year Ended _____

2. _____

_____

_____

_____

_____

_____

_____

_____

_____

_____

_____

_____

_____

_____

3. _____

_____

_____

_____

_____

_____

_____

_____

This Page Not Used.

PROBLEM 20-5 ___

1.

	SIZE			TOTAL
	S	M	L	

Variable Costing Income Statement

2. _____

PROBLEM 20-5 ___, Concluded

3.

	Variable Costing Income Statement		

	SIZE		TOTAL
	S	L	

4. _____

_____

_____

_____

_____

PROBLEM 20-6 ___

1.

Contribution Margin Analysis		

PROBLEM 20-6 ___, Concluded

2. _____

_____

_____

_____

_____

_____

_____

_____

_____

_____

_____

_____

_____

_____

_____

_____

_____

_____

_____

_____

_____

_____

_____

_____

_____

_____

_____

_____

_____

_____

_____

_____

_____

EXERCISE 21-1

a.

	A	B	C	D	E
1	KATHERINE MALLOY				
2	Cash Budget				
3	For the Four Months Ending December 31, 2016				
4		September	October	November	December
5					
6					
7					
8					
9					
10					
11					
12					
13					
14					
15					
16					
17					
18					
19					
20					
21					
22					
23					
24					
25					
26					
27					
28					

b. _____

_____

_____

EXERCISE 21-1, Concluded

c. _____

_____

_____

_____

_____

_____

_____

_____

_____

_____

_____

_____

_____

_____

_____

_____

_____

_____

_____

_____

_____

_____

EXERCISE 21-2

	A	B	C	D
1	CLOUD PRODUCTIVITY INC.			
2	Flexible Selling and Administrative Expenses Budget			
3	For the Month Ending March 31, 2016			
4				
5				
6				
7				
8				
9				
10				
11				
12				
13				
14				
15				
16				
17				
18				
19				
20				
21				
22				
23				
24				
25				
26				
27				
28				

EXERCISE 21-3

a.

	A	B	C	D
1	RODRIGUEZ COMPANY—MACHINING DEPARTMENT			
2	Flexible Production Budget			
3	For the Three Months Ending March 31, 2016			
4		January	February	March
5				
6				
7				
8				
9				
10				
11				
12				
13				
14				
15				
16				
17				
18				
19				
20				
21				
22				
23				
24				
25				

_____

_____

_____

_____

_____

EXERCISE 21-3, Concluded

b.

	JANUARY	FEBRUARY	MARCH

_____

_____

_____

_____

_____

_____

_____

_____

_____

_____

_____

_____

_____

_____

_____

EXERCISE 21-4

	A	B	C	D
1	STEELCASE INC.—ASSEMBLY DEPARTMENT			
2	Flexible Production Budget			
3	August 2016			
4	(assumed data)			
5				
6				
7				
8				
9				
10				
11				
12				
13				
14				
15				
16				
17				
18				
19				

EXERCISE 21-5

	A	B	C
1	TRUE TAB INC.		
2	Production Budget		
3	For the Month Ending July 31, 2017		
4		Units	
5		Small Scale	Large Scale
6			
7			
8			
9			
10			
11			
12			
13			

EXERCISE 21-6

a.

	A	B	C	D
1	SOUNDLAB INC.			
2	Sales Budget			
3	For the Month Ending September 30, 2016			
4	Product and Area	Unit Sales Volume	Unit Selling Price	Total Sales
5				
6				
7				
8				
9				
10				
11				
12				
13				
14				

EXERCISE 21-6, Concluded

b.

	A	B	C
1	SOUNDLAB INC.		
2	Production Budget		
3	For the Month Ended September 30, 2016		
4		Units	
5		Model DL	Model XL
6			
7			
8			
9			
10			
11			
12			
13			

EXERCISE 21-7

	A	B	C	D
1	ROLLINS AND COHEN, CPAs			
2	Professional Fees Earned Budget			
3	For the Year Ending December 31, 2016			
4		Billable Hours	Hourly Rate	Total Revenue
5				
6				
7				
8				
9				
10				
11				
12				
13				
14				
15				
16				
17				
18				
19				
20				
21				
22				

EXERCISE 21-8

	A	B	C
1	ROLLINS AND COHEN, CPAs		
2	Professional Labor Cost Budget		
3	For the Year Ending December 31, 2016		
4		Staff	Partners
5			
6			
7			
8			
9			
10			
11			
12			

EXERCISE 21-9

	A	B	C	D	E
1	ROMANO'S FROZEN PIZZA INC.				
2	Direct Materials Purchases Budget				
3	For the Month Ending September 30, 2016				
4		Dough	Tomato	Cheese	Total
5					
6					
7					
8					
9					
10					
11					
12					
13					
14					
15					
16					
17					
18					
19					
20					
21					
22					
23					
24					
25					
26					

EXERCISE 21-10

	A	B	C	D
1	COCA-COLA ENTERPRISES—WAKEFIELD PLANT			
2	Direct Materials Purchases Budget			
3	For the Month Ending May 31, 2016			
4	(assumed data)			
5		Concentrate	2-Liter Bottles	Carbonated Water
6				
7				
8				
9				
10				
11				
12				
13				
14				
15				

Supporting calculations:

EXERCISE 21-11

	A	B	C	D
1	SAFETY GRIP COMPANY			
2	Direct Materials Purchases Budget			
3	For the Year Ending December 31, 2016			
4		Rubber	Steel Belts	Total
5				
6				
7				
8				
9				
10				
11				
12				
13				
14				
15				
16				
17				
18				
19				
20				
21				
22				
23				
24				
25				
26				
27				
28				

EXERCISE 21-12

	A	B	C
1	ACE RACKET COMPANY		
2	Direct Labor Cost Budget		
3	For the Month Ending July 31, 2016		
4		Forming Department	Assembly Department
5			
6			
7			
8			
9			
10			
11			
12			
13			
14			
15			
16			
17			
18			

EXERCISE 21-13

	A	B	C
1	AMBASSADOR SUITES INC.		
2	Direct Labor Cost Budget		
3	For a Weekday or a Weekend Day		
4		Weekday	Weekend Day
5			
6			
7			
8			
9			
10			
11			
12			
13			
14			
15			
16			
17			
18			
19			
20			
21			
22			
23			
24			
25			
26			
27			
28			
29			
30			

EXERCISE 21-14

a.

	A	B	C
1	LEVI STRAUSS & CO.		
2	Production Budget		
3	May 2016		
4	(assumed data)		
5		Dockers®	501 Jeans®
6			
7			
8			
9			
10			
11			
12			

EXERCISE 21-14, Concluded

b.

	A	B	C	D	E	F
1			LEVI STRAUSS & CO.			
2			Direct Labor Cost Budget			
3			May 2016			
4			(assumed data)			
5		Inseam	Outerseam	Pockets	Zipper	Total
6						
7						
8						
9						
10						
11						
12						
13						
14						
15						
16						
17						
18						
19						
20						
21						
22						
23						
24						
25						
26						
27						
28						
29						
30						
31						
32						

EXERCISE 21-15

	A	B	C
1	SWEET TOOTH CANDY COMPANY		
2	Factory Overhead Cost Budget		
3	For the Month Ending August 31, 2016		
4			
5			
6			
7			
8			
9			
10			
11			
12			
13			
14			
15			
16			
17			
18			
19			
20			
21			
22			

EXERCISE 21-16

	A	B	C	D
1	DELAWARE CHEMICAL COMPANY			
2	Cost of Goods Sold Budget			
3	For the Month Ending June 30, 2017			
4				
5				
6				
7				
8				
9				
10				
11				
12				
13				
14				
15				
16				
17				
18				
19				
20				
21				
22				
23				
24				
25				
26				
27				
28				
29				
30				
31				
32				
33				
34				
35				
36				

EXERCISE 21-17

	A	B	C	D
1	**MINGWARE CERAMICS INC.**			
2	**Cost of Goods Sold Budget**			
3	**For the Month Ending September 30, 2016**			
4				
5				
6				
7				
8				
9				
10				
11				
12				
13				
14				
15				
16				
17				
18				
19				
20				
21				
22				
23				
24				
25				
26				
27				
28				
29				
30				
31				
32				

EXERCISE 21-18

	A	B	C	D
1	PET PLACE SUPPLIES INC.			
2	Schedule of Collections from Sales			
3	For the Three Months Ending July 31, 2016			
4		May	June	July
5				
6				
7				
8				
9				
10				
11				
12				
13				
14				
15				
16				
17				
18				
19				
20				
21				
22				
23				
24				
25				
26				
27				

EXERCISE 21-19

	A	B	C	D
1	OFFICEMART INC.			
2	Schedule of Collections from Sales			
3	For the Three Months Ending December 31, 2016			
4		October	November	December
5				
6				
7				
8				
9				
10				
11				
12				
13				
14				
15				
16				
17				
18				
19				
20				
21				
22				
23				
24				
25				
26				
27				
28				
29				
30				
31				
32				

EXERCISE 21-20

	A	B	C	D
1	HORIZON FINANCIAL INC.			
2	Schedule of Cash Payments for Selling and Administrative Expenses			
3	For the Three Months Ending May 31, 2016			
4		March	April	May
5				
6				
7				
8				
9				
10				
11				
12				
13				
14				
15				
16				
17				
18				
19				
20				
21				
22				

EXERCISE 21-21

	A	B	C	D
1	EASTGATE PHYSICAL THERAPY INC.			
2	Schedule of Cash Payments for Operations			
3	For the Three Months Ending March 31, 2017			
4		January	February	March
5				
6				
7				
8				
9				
10				
11				
12				
13				
14				
15				
16				
17				
18				
19				
20				
21				
22				

EXERCISE 21-22

	A	B	C	D	E
1	OMICRON INC.				
2	Capital Expenditures Budget				
3	For the Four Years Ending December 31, 2016–2019				
4		2016	2017	2018	2019
5					
6					
7					
8					
9					
10					
11					
12					

This Page Not Used.

PROBLEM 21-1 ___

1.

	UNIT SALES, YEAR ENDED 2016		INCREASE (DECREASE) ACTUAL OVER BUDGET	
	BUDGET	ACTUAL SALES	AMOUNT	PERCENT

2.

	2016 ACTUAL UNITS	PERCENTAGE INCREASE (DECREASE)	2017 BUDGETED UNITS (ROUNDED)

PROBLEM 21-1 ___, Concluded

3.

	A	B	C	D
1				
2	Sales Budget			
3				
4	Product and Area	Unit Sales Volume	Unit Selling Price	Total Sales
5				
6				
7				
8				
9				
10				
11				
12				
13				
14				
15				
16				
17				
18				
19				
20				

PROBLEM 21-2 ___

1.

	A	B	C	D
1				
2	Sales Budget			
3				
4	Product and Area	Unit Sales Volume	Unit Selling Price	Total Sales
5				
6				
7				
8				
9				
10				
11				
12				
13				
14				
15				
16				
17				
18				

2.

	A	B	C
1			
2	Production Budget		
3			
4		Units	
5			
6			
7			
8			
9			
10			
11			
12			
13			
14			
15			
16			

PROBLEM 21-2 ___ , Continued

3.

	A	B	C	D	E	F
1						
2		Direct Materials Purchases Budget				
3						
4						
5						
6						
7						
8						
9						
10						
11						
12						
13						
14						
15						
16						
17						
18						
19						
20						
21						
22						
23						
24						
25						
26						
27						
28						
29						
30						
31						
32						
33						
34						
35						
36						
37						
38						
39						
40						
41						
42						

PROBLEM 21-2 ___ , Concluded

4.

	A	B	C	D	E
1					
2		**Direct Labor Cost Budget**			
3					
4		Department	Department	Department	Total
5					
6					
7					
8					
9					
10					
11					
12					
13					
14					
15					
16					
17					
18					
19					
20					
21					
22					
23					
24					
25					
26					
27					
28					
29					
30					
31					
32					

This Page Not Used.

PROBLEM 21-3 ___

1.

	A	B	C	D
1				
2	Sales Budget			
3				
4		Unit Sales Volume	Unit Selling Price	Total Sales
5				
6				
7				
8				
9				
10				

2.

	A	B	C
1			
2	Production Budget		
3			
4		Units	
5			
6			
7			
8			
9			
10			
11			
12			
13			
14			
15			

PROBLEM 21-3 ___, Continued

3.

	A	B	C	D
1				
2	**Direct Materials Purchases Budget**			
3				
4				**Total**
5				
6				
7				
8				
9				
10				
11				
12				
13				
14				
15				
16				
17				
18				
19				
20				
21				
22				
23				
24				
25				
26				

PROBLEM 21-3 ___, Continued

4.

	A	B	C	D
1				
2	**Direct Labor Cost Budget**			
3				
4		Department	Department	Total
5				
6				
7				
8				
9				
10				
11				
12				
13				
14				
15				
16				
17				
18				
19				
20				

5.

	A	B
1		
2	**Factory Overhead Cost Budget**	
3		
4		
5		
6		
7		
8		
9		
10		

PROBLEM 21-3 ___, Continued

6.

	A	B	C	D
1				
2	Cost of Goods Sold Budget			
3				
4				
5				
6				
7				
8				
9				
10				
11				
12				
13				
14				
15				
16				
17				
18				
19				
20				
21				
22				
23				
24				
25				
26				
27				
28				
29				
30				
31				
32				
33				
34				

PROBLEM 21-3 ___, Continued

Supporting calculations:

PROBLEM 21-3 ___, Continued

7.

	A	B	C
1			
2	**Selling and Administrative Expenses Budget**		
3			
4			
5			
6			
7			
8			
9			
10			
11			
12			
13			
14			
15			
16			
17			
18			
19			
20			
21			
22			
23			
24			

PROBLEM 21-3 ___, Concluded

8.

	A	B	C
1			
2	Budgeted Income Statement		
3			
4			
5			
6			
7			
8			
9			
10			
11			
12			
13			
14			
15			
16			
17			
18			
19			
20			

This Page Not Used.

PROBLEM 21-4 ___

1.

	A	B	C	D
1				
2	Cash Budget			
3				
4				
5				
6				
7				
8				
9				
10				
11				
12				
13				
14				
15				
16				
17				
18				
19				
20				
21				
22				
23				
24				
25				
26				
27				
28				
29				
30				

PROBLEM 21-4 ___, Continued

Computations:

PROBLEM 21-4 ___, Concluded

2. _____

_____

_____

_____

_____

_____

_____

_____

_____

_____

_____

This Page Not Used.

PROBLEM 21-5 ___

1.

	A	B	C	D
1				
2	Budgeted Income Statement			
3				
4				
5				
6				
7				
8				
9				
10				
11				
12				
13				
14				
15				
16				
17				
18				
19				
20				
21				
22				
23				
24				
25				
26				
27				
28				
29				
30				
31				
32				
33				
34				
35				
36				
37				
38				
39				
40				
41				
42				

PROBLEM 21-5 ___, Continued

2.

	A	B	C	D
1				
2	Budgeted Balance Sheet			
3				
4				
5				
6				
7				
8				
9				
10				
11				
12				
13				
14				
15				
16				
17				
18				
19				
20				
21				
22				
23				
24				
25				
26				
27				
28				

PROBLEM 21-5 ___, Concluded

Supporting calculations:

This Page Not Used.

EXERCISE 22-1

Ingredient	Quantity	×	Price	Total
		×		
		×		
		×		

_____

_____

_____

_____

_____

_____

EXERCISE 22-2

a.

b. _____

_____

_____

_____

_____

_____

_____

_____

_____

EXERCISE 22-3

a.

	A	B
1	GENIE IN A BOTTLE COMPANY	
2	Manufacturing Cost Budget	
3	For the Month Ended July 31	
4		Standard Cost at Planned Volume (400,000 Bottles)
5		
6		
7		
8		
9		
10		
11		
12		
13		
14		
15		
16		

b.

	A	B	C	D
1	GENIE IN A BOTTLE COMPANY			
2	Manufacturing Costs—Budget Performance Report			
3	For the Month Ended July 31			
4		Actual Costs	Standard Cost at Actual Volume (406,000 Bottles)	Cost Variance— (Favorable) Unfavorable
5				
6				
7				
8				
9				
10				
11				
12				
13				
14				
15				
16				
17				
18				

EXERCISE 22-3, Concluded

c. _____

_____

_____

_____

_____

EXERCISE 22-4

a. Price variance: _____

_____

_____

_____

_____

_____

_____

_____

Quantity variance: _____

_____

_____

_____

_____

_____

_____

Total direct materials cost variance: _____

_____

_____

_____

_____

_____

_____

EXERCISE 22-4, Concluded

b. _____

_____

_____

_____

_____

_____

_____

_____

_____

_____

_____

_____

_____

_____

_____

_____

_____

_____

_____

_____

_____

_____

_____

_____

_____

_____

EXERCISE 22-5

Price variance: _____

_____

_____

_____

_____

_____

_____

_____

Quantity variance: _____

_____

_____

_____

_____

_____

_____

Total direct materials cost variance: _____

_____

_____

_____

_____

_____

_____

_____

EXERCISE 22-6

Alternate solution:

Proof:

_____

_____

_____

_____

_____

_____

_____

_____

_____

EXERCISE 22-7

a.

b.

EXERCISE 22-8

a. Rate variance: _____

_____

_____

_____

_____

_____

_____

Time variance: _____

_____

_____

_____

_____

_____

_____

Total direct labor cost variance: _____

_____

_____

_____

_____

_____

_____

b. _____

_____

_____

_____

_____

_____

_____

_____

_____

_____

EXERCISE 22-9

a. Rate variance: _____

_____

_____

_____

_____

_____

_____

Time variance: _____

_____

_____

_____

_____

_____

_____

Total direct labor cost variance: _____

_____

_____

_____

_____

_____

_____

b. Debit to Work in Process: _____

EXERCISE 22-10

a. **(1)** Cutting Department

Rate variance: _____

_____

_____

_____

_____

_____

_____

Time variance: _____

_____

_____

_____

_____

_____

_____

Total direct labor cost variance: _____

_____

_____

_____

_____

_____

EXERCISE 22-10, Continued

(2) Sewing Department

Rate variance: _____

_____

_____

_____

_____

_____

_____

_____

Time variance: _____

_____

_____

_____

_____

_____

_____

_____

Total direct labor cost variance: _____

_____

_____

_____

_____

_____

_____

_____

EXERCISE 22-10, Concluded

b. _____

_____

_____

_____

_____

_____

_____

_____

_____

_____

_____

_____

_____

_____

_____

EXERCISE 22-11

a. _____

_____

b.

c.

_____

_____

_____

_____

_____

EXERCISE 22-12

a. _____

_____

_____

_____

_____

_____

_____

_____

_____

_____

_____

_____

_____

_____

_____

_____

_____

_____

_____

b. _____

_____

_____

_____

_____

_____

_____

EXERCISE 22-13

a. Rate variance: _____

_____

_____

_____

_____

_____

_____

Time variance: _____

_____

_____

_____

_____

_____

_____

Total direct labor cost variance: _____

_____

_____

_____

_____

_____

_____

_____

EXERCISE 22-13, Concluded

b. _____

_____

_____

_____

_____

_____

_____

_____

_____

_____

_____

_____

_____

_____

_____

_____

_____

_____

EXERCISE 22-14

Step 1: _____

_____

_____

_____

_____

_____

_____

_____

_____

_____

_____

_____

_____

_____

_____

_____

_____

_____

_____

_____

_____

_____

_____

_____

_____

_____

Step 2: _____

_____

_____

EXERCISE 22-14, Concluded

Step 3: _____

_____

_____

EXERCISE 22-15

	A	B	C	D
1	LENO MANUFACTURING COMPANY			
2	Factory Overhead Cost Budget—Press Department			
3	For the Month Ended November 30			
4				
5				
6				
7				
8				
9				
10				
11				
12				
13				
14				
15				
16				
17				
18				
19				
20				
21				
22				
23				
24				

EXERCISE 22-16

a.

	A	B	C	D
1	WIKI WIKI COMPANY			
2	Monthly Factory Overhead Cost Budget—Fabrication Department			
3				
4				
5				
6				
7				
8				
9				
10				

b. Overhead applied to actual production:

Supporting calculations:

EXERCISE 22-17

Variable factory overhead controllable variance:

Fixed factory overhead volume variance:

Total factory overhead cost variance:

EXERCISE 22-17, Concluded

Alternative Computation of Overhead Variances:

EXERCISE 22-18

a. Controllable variance:

b. Volume variance:

Total factory overhead cost variance:

EXERCISE 22-18, Concluded

Alternative Computation of Overhead Variances:

EXERCISE 22-19

_____
_____
_____
_____
_____
_____
_____
_____
_____
_____

Correct Determination of Factory Overhead Cost Variances:

EXERCISE 22-19, Concluded

Alternative Computation of Overhead Variances:

EXERCISE 22-20

	A	B	C	D	E
1	TANNIN PRODUCTS INC.				
2	Factory Overhead Cost Variance Report—Trim Department				
3	For the Month Ended July 31				
4	Productive capacity for the month				
5	Actual productive capacity used for the month				
6					
7		Budget (at actual production)	Actual	Variances	
8					
9				Favorable	Unfavorable
10					
11					
12					
13					
14					
15					
16					
17					
18					
19					
20					
21					
22					
23					
24					
25					
26					
27					
28					
29					
30					
31					
32					
33					
34					
35					
36					
37					
38					
39					
40					
41					
42					
43					
44					
45					
46					

EXERCISE 22-20, Concluded

Alternative Computation of Overhead Variances:

EXERCISE 22-21

a. and b.

JOURNAL   PAGE

	DATE	DESCRIPTION	POST. REF.	DEBIT	CREDIT	
1						1
2						2
3						3
4						4
5						5
6						6
7						7
8						8

EXERCISE 22-22

JOURNAL   PAGE

	DATE	DESCRIPTION	POST. REF.	DEBIT	CREDIT	
1						1
2						2
3						3
4						4
5						5
6						6
7						7
8						8
9						9
10						10
11						11
12						12

EXERCISE 22-23

		Income Statement		

	FAVORABLE	UNFAVORABLE	

EXERCISE 22-24

a. and b.

	Input Measure	Output Measure	Explanation
Average computer response time to customer "clicks"			
Dollar amount of returned goods			
Elapsed time between customer order and product delivery			
Maintenance dollars divided by hardware investment			
Number of customer complaints divided by the number of orders			
Number of misfilled orders divided by the number of orders			
Number of orders per warehouse employee			
Number of page faults or errors due to software programming errors			
Number of software fixes per week			
Server (computer) downtime			
Training dollars per programmer			

EXERCISE 22-25

a. Input Measures: _____

_____

_____

_____

_____

_____

_____

_____

_____

Output Measures: _____

_____

_____

_____

_____

_____

_____

_____

_____

_____

_____

_____

_____

b. _____

_____

_____

_____

_____

_____

_____

_____

_____

_____

_____

_____

_____

PROBLEM 22-1 ___

a.

b.   **Direct Materials Cost Variance**

Price variance: _____

_____

_____

_____

_____

_____

_____

_____

Quantity variance: _____

_____

_____

_____

_____

_____

_____

Total direct materials cost variance: _____

_____

_____

_____

_____

_____

_____

_____

PROBLEM 22-1 ___, Concluded

c.   **<u>Direct Labor Cost Variance</u>**

Rate variance: _____

_____

_____

_____

_____

_____

_____

Time variance: _____

_____

_____

_____

_____

_____

_____

Total direct labor cost variance: _____

_____

_____

_____

_____

_____

_____

_____

PROBLEM 22-2 ___

1. a.

			TOTAL

PROBLEM 22-2 ___, Continued

b.

			TOTAL	

PROBLEM 22-2 ___, Concluded

2. _____

_____

_____

_____

_____

_____

_____

_____

_____

_____

_____

_____

_____

_____

This Page Not Used.

PROBLEM 22-3 ___

a.

<u>Direct Materials Cost Variance</u>

Price variance: _____

_____

_____

_____

_____

_____

_____

Quantity variance: _____

_____

_____

_____

_____

_____

_____

Total direct materials cost variance: _____

_____

_____

_____

_____

_____

_____

PROBLEM 22-3 ___, Continued

b.   <u>**Direct Labor Cost Variance**</u>

Rate variance: _____

_____

_____

_____

_____

_____

_____

Time variance: _____

_____

_____

_____

_____

_____

_____

Total direct labor cost variance: _____

_____

_____

_____

_____

_____

_____

_____

PROBLEM 22-3 ___, Continued

c. <u>Factory Overhead Cost Variance</u>

PROBLEM 22-3 ___, Concluded

Alternative Computation of Overhead Variances:

PROBLEM 22-4 ___

	A	B	C	D	E
1					
2	Factory Overhead Cost Variance Report—_____ Department				
3					
4	Normal capacity for the month				
5	Actual production for the month				
6					
7				Variances	
8		Budget	Actual	Favorable	Unfavorable
9					
10					
11					
12					
13					
14					
15					
16					
17					
18					
19					
20					
21					
22					
23					
24					
25					
26					
27					
28					
29					
30					
31					
32					
33					
34					
35					
36					
37					
38					
39					
40					
41					
42					
43					
44					
45					

PROBLEM 22-4 ___, Concluded

Alternative Computation of Overhead Variances:

PROBLEM 22-5 ___

1.

2.

PROBLEM 22-5 ___, Continued

3.

4.

PROBLEM 22-5 ___, Concluded

5.

6.

This Page Not Used.

COMPREHENSIVE PROBLEM 5

Part A

1. _____

_____

_____

_____

_____

_____

_____

_____

_____

_____

_____

_____

_____

2.

3.

4. _____

_____

_____

_____

_____

COMPREHENSIVE PROBLEM 5, Continued

Part B

5.

	CASES
Production Budget	

6.

	CREAM BASE (OZS.)	NATURAL OILS (OZS.)	BOTTLES (BOTTLES)	TOTAL
Direct Materials Purchases Budget				

COMPREHENSIVE PROBLEM 5, Continued

7.

	MIXING	FILLING	TOTAL
Direct Labor Budget			

8.

Factory Overhead Budget			

COMPREHENSIVE PROBLEM 5, Continued

9.

Budgeted Income Statement			

COMPREHENSIVE PROBLEM 5, Continued

Part C

10. Direct Materials Price Variance:

	CREAM BASE	NATURAL OILS	BOTTLES

COMPREHENSIVE PROBLEM 5, Continued

Direct Materials Quantity Variance:

	CREAM BASE	NATURAL OILS	BOTTLES	

COMPREHENSIVE PROBLEM 5, Continued

11. Direct Labor Rate Variance:

	MIXING DEPARTMENT	FILLING DEPARTMENT

_____

_____

_____

_____

_____

_____

_____

_____

_____

COMPREHENSIVE PROBLEM 5, Continued

Direct Labor Time Variance:

	MIXING DEPARTMENT	FILLING DEPARTMENT	

COMPREHENSIVE PROBLEM 5, Continued

12. Factory Overhead Controllable Variance:

13. Factory Overhead Volume Variance:

COMPREHENSIVE PROBLEM 5, Continued

Alternative Computation of Overhead Variances:

COMPREHENSIVE PROBLEM 5, Concluded

14. _____

_____

_____

_____

_____

_____

_____

_____

_____

_____

_____

_____

_____

This Page Not Used.

EXERCISE 23-1

a.

Saskatoon Company
Budget Performance Report—Vice President, Production
For the Month Ended June 30, 2016

Plant	Budget	Actual	Over Budget	Under Budget
Eastern Region	$936,000	$933,750		$2,250
Central Region	669,600	666,000		3,600
Western Region	(g) _____	(h) _____	(i) $ _____	_____
	(j) $ _____	(k) $ _____	(l) $ _____	$5,850

Saskatoon Company
Budget Performance Report—Manager, Western Region Plant
For the Month Ended June 30, 2016

Department	Budget	Actual	Over Budget	Under Budget
Chip Fabrication	(a) $ _____	(b) $ _____	(c) $ _____	
Electronic Assembly	191,250	194,040	2,520	
Final Assembly	308,250	307,440	_____	$810
	(d) $ _____	(e) $ _____	(f) $ _____	$810

Saskatoon Company
Budget Performance Report—Supervisor, Chip Fabrication
For the Month Ended June 30, 2016

Cost	Budget	Actual	Over Budget	Under Budget
Factory wages	$ 59,940	$ 61,500	$1,560	
Materials	156,600	155,520		$1,080
Power and light	8,640	10,260	1,620	
Maintenance	15,120	16,560	1,440	_____
	$240,300	$243,840	$4,620	$1,080

EXERCISE 23-1, Concluded

b. _____

_____

_____

_____

_____

_____

_____

_____

_____

_____

_____

_____

_____

_____

_____

_____

_____

_____

_____

_____

_____

EXERCISE 23-2

Divisional Income Statements

	COMMERCIAL DIVISION	RESIDENTIAL DIVISION	

EXERCISE 23-3

a. Legal: _____
_____

b. Duplication services: _____
_____

c. Electronic data processing: _____
_____

d. Central purchasing: _____
_____

e. Telecommunications: _____
_____

f. Accounts receivable: _____
_____

EXERCISE 23-4

a. Accounts Receivable: _____
b. Central Purchasing: _____
c. Computer Support: _____
d. Conferences: _____
e. Employee Travel: _____
f. Payroll Accounting: _____
g. Telecommunications: _____
h. Training: _____

EXERCISE 23-5

a.

	RESIDENTIAL	COMMERCIAL	GOVERNMENT CONTRACT	TOTAL	

EXERCISE 23-5, Continued

b.

	RESIDENTIAL	COMMERCIAL	GOVERNMENT CONTRACT	TOTAL

EXERCISE 23-5, Concluded

c. _____

_____

_____

_____

_____

_____

_____

_____

_____

_____

_____

_____

_____

_____

_____

_____

_____

_____

EXERCISE 23-6

a. Help desk: _____

_____

_____

Network center: _____

_____

_____

Electronic mail: _____

_____

_____

Local voice support: _____

_____

_____

b. Help desk: _____

_____

_____

Network center: _____

_____

_____

Electronic mail: _____

_____

_____

Local voice support: _____

_____

_____

EXERCISE 23-7

Divisional Income Statements

	CONSUMER DIVISION		COMMERCIAL DIVISION	

Supporting calculations:

_____

_____

_____

_____

_____

_____

_____

_____

_____

_____

EXERCISE 23-8

a. _____

_____

_____

_____

_____

_____

_____

_____

_____

_____

_____

_____

_____

_____

_____

_____

EXERCISE 23-8, Concluded

b.

	Divisional Income Statements			

	PASSENGER DIVISION		CARGO DIVISION	

Supporting calculations:

_____

_____

_____

_____

_____

_____

_____

_____

_____

_____

_____

_____

_____

_____

_____

_____

_____

EXERCISE 23-9

Divisional Income Statements

	WINTER SPORTS DIVISION	SUMMER SPORTS DIVISION

EXERCISE 23-9, Concluded

Supporting Schedule:

_____

_____

_____

_____

_____

_____

_____

_____

_____

_____

_____

_____

_____

EXERCISE 23-10

a. Retail Division: _____

Commercial Division: _____

Internet Division: _____

b. _____

EXERCISE 23-11

a.

	RETAIL DIVISION	COMMERCIAL DIVISION	INTERNET DIVISION

b. _____

EXERCISE 23-12

Rate of Return on Investment	=	Profit Margin	×	Investment Turnover
13.2%	=	6%	×	**(a)** _____
(b) _____	=	10%	×	1.80
10.5%	=	**(c)** _____	×	1.50
15%	=	5%	×	**(d)** _____
(e) _____	=	12%	×	1.10

EXERCISE 23-13

a. _____

_____

_____

_____

_____

_____

_____

_____

_____

_____

_____

_____

_____

_____

b. _____

_____

_____

_____

_____

_____

_____

_____

_____

_____

_____

_____

_____

_____

_____

_____

_____

_____

_____

_____

_____

EXERCISE 23-14

a. _____

_____

_____

Media Networks: _____

_____

_____

_____

_____

_____

Parks and Resorts: _____

_____

_____

_____

_____

_____

Studio Entertainment: _____

_____

_____

_____

_____

_____

Consumer Products: _____

_____

_____

_____

_____

_____

EXERCISE 23-14, Concluded

b. _____

_____

_____

_____

_____

_____

_____

_____

_____

_____

_____

_____

_____

_____

_____

EXERCISE 23-15

Invested Assets	Income from Operations	Rate of Return on Investment	Minimum Rate of Return	Minimum Acceptable Income from Operations	Residual Income
$925,000	$185,000	(a) _____	15%	(b) $ _____	(c) $ _____
$775,000	(d) $ _____	(e) _____	(f) _____	$93,000	$23,250
$450,000	(g) $ _____	18%	(h) _____	$58,500	(i) $ _____
$610,000	$97,600	(j) _____	12%	(k) $ _____	(l) $ _____

Calculations:

(a) _____

(b) _____

(c) _____

(d) _____

(e) _____

(f) _____

(g) _____

(h) _____

(i) _____

(j) _____

(k) _____

(l) _____

EXERCISE 23-16

a.

	Sales	Income from Operations	Invested Assets	Rate of Return on Investment	Profit Margin	Investment Turnover
North	$860,000	(a) $_____	(b) $_____	17.5%	7.0%	(c) _____
South	(d) $_____	$51,300	(e) $_____	(f) _____	4.5%	3.8
East	$1,020,000	(g) $_____	$680,000	15.0%	(h) _____	(i) _____
West	$1,120,000	$89,600	$560,000	(j) _____	(k) _____	(l) _____

Calculations:

(a) _____

(b) _____

(c) _____

(d) _____

(e) _____

(f) _____

(g) _____

(h) _____

(i) _____

(j) _____

(k) _____

(l) _____

b. North Division: _____

_____

South Division: _____

_____

East Division: _____

_____

West Division: _____

_____

c. (1) _____

(2) _____

EXERCISE 23-17

a. _____

_____

_____

_____

Hotel Ownership: _____

_____

_____

_____

_____

_____

Vacation Ownership: _____

_____

_____

_____

_____

_____

b.

	HOTEL OWNERSHIP	VACATION OWNERSHIP

EXERCISE 23-17, Concluded

c. _____

_____

_____

_____

_____

_____

_____

_____

_____

_____

_____

_____

_____

_____

_____

_____

_____

_____

_____

_____

_____

_____

_____

_____

_____

_____

_____

_____

EXERCISE 23-18

Average card member spending: _____

_____

Cards in force: _____

_____

Earnings growth: _____

_____

Hours of credit consultant training: _____

_____

Investment in information technology: _____

_____

Number of card choices: _____

_____

Number of Internet features: _____

_____

Number of merchant signings: _____

_____

Number of new card launches: _____

_____

Return on equity: _____

_____

Revenue growth: _____

_____

EXERCISE 23-19

_____

_____

_____

_____

_____

_____

_____

_____

_____

_____

_____

_____

_____

_____

_____

_____

_____

_____

_____

_____

_____

_____

_____

_____

_____

_____

_____

_____

_____

_____

_____

_____

_____

_____

_____

_____

_____

_____

EXERCISE 23-20

a. _____

_____

_____

_____

_____

_____

_____

b. _____

_____

_____

_____

_____

_____

_____

c. _____

_____

_____

_____

_____

_____

_____

EXERCISE 23-21

a. _____

_____

_____

_____

_____

_____

_____

_____

_____

_____

_____

_____

b. _____

_____

_____

_____

_____

_____

_____

_____

_____

_____

_____

_____

EXERCISE 23-21, Concluded

c. _____

d. _____

PROBLEM 23-1 ___

1.

		BUDGET	ACTUAL	OVER BUDGET	UNDER BUDGET
Budget Performance Report — _____

	BUDGET	ACTUAL	OVER BUDGET	UNDER BUDGET

2. _____

_____

_____

_____

_____

_____

_____

_____

_____

_____

_____

_____

_____

_____

_____

_____

_____

This Page Not Used.

PROBLEM 23-2 ___

1.

Divisional Income Statements

Supporting schedule:

PROBLEM 23-2 ___, Concluded

2. _____

_____

_____

_____

_____

_____

_____

_____

_____

_____

_____

_____

3. _____

_____

_____

_____

_____

_____

_____

_____

_____

_____

_____

_____

_____

_____

_____

_____

_____

_____

_____

PROBLEM 23-3 ___

1.

Divisional Income Statements			

PROBLEM 23-3 ___, Continued

2. _____

_____

_____

_____

_____

_____

_____

_____

_____

_____

_____

_____

_____

_____

_____

_____

_____

_____

_____

_____

_____

_____

_____

_____

_____

_____

_____

_____

_____

_____

_____

_____

_____

_____

_____

_____

PROBLEM 23-3 ___ , Concluded

3. _____

_____

_____

_____

_____

_____

_____

_____

_____

_____

_____

_____

_____

_____

_____

_____

_____

This Page Not Used.

PROBLEM 23-4 ___

1. _____

_____

_____

_____

_____

_____

_____

_____

_____

_____

_____

_____

_____

_____

_____

_____

_____

_____

_____

2.

Estimated Income Statements

	PROPOSAL 1	PROPOSAL 2	PROPOSAL 3

PROBLEM 23-4 ___, Continued

3. _____

_____

_____

_____

_____

_____

_____

_____

_____

_____

_____

_____

_____

_____

_____

_____

_____

_____

_____

_____

_____

_____

_____

_____

_____

_____

_____

4. _____

_____

_____

PROBLEM 23-4 ___, Concluded

5. _____

_____

_____

_____

_____

_____

_____

_____

_____

_____

_____

_____

_____

_____

_____

_____

_____

_____

_____

_____

_____

This Page Not Used.

PROBLEM 23-5 ___

1.

	Divisional Income Statements		

PROBLEM 23-5 ___, Continued

2. _____

_____

_____

_____

_____

_____

_____

_____

_____

_____

_____

_____

_____

_____

_____

_____

_____

_____

_____

_____

_____

_____

_____

_____

_____

_____

_____

_____

3. _____

_____

_____

_____

_____

PROBLEM 23-5 ___, Concluded

4. _____

_____

_____

_____

_____

_____

_____

_____

_____

_____

_____

_____

_____

_____

_____

_____

_____

_____

_____

_____

_____

_____

_____

_____

_____

_____

_____

_____

_____

_____

This Page Not Used.

PROBLEM 23-6 ___

1. _____

_____

_____

_____

_____

PROBLEM 23-6 ___, Continued

2. _____

_____

_____

_____

_____

_____

_____

_____

_____

_____

_____

_____

_____

_____

_____

_____

_____

_____

_____

_____

_____

_____

_____

_____

_____

_____

_____

_____

_____

_____

_____

_____

_____

_____

_____

_____

_____

_____

_____

PROBLEM 23-6 ___, Continued

3.

			Divisional Income Statements

			TOTAL

PROBLEM 23-6 ___, Continued

4. _____

_____

_____

_____

_____

_____

_____

_____

_____

_____

_____

_____

_____

_____

_____

_____

_____

_____

_____

_____

_____

_____

_____

_____

_____

_____

_____

_____

_____

_____

_____

_____

_____

_____

_____

_____

PROBLEM 23-6 ___, Concluded

5. a. _____

_____

_____

_____

_____

_____

_____

_____

_____

b. _____

_____

_____

_____

_____

_____

_____

_____

_____

This Page Not Used.

EXERCISE 24-1

a.

	LEASE MACHINERY (ALTERNATIVE 1)	SELL MACHINERY (ALTERNATIVE 2)	DIFFERENTIAL EFFECT ON INCOME (ALTERNATIVE 2)
Lease Machinery (Alternative 1) or Sell Machinery (Alternative 2)			

b. _____

EXERCISE 24-2

	LEASE EQUIPMENT (ALTERNATIVE 1)	BUY EQUIPMENT (ALTERNATIVE 2)	DIFFERENTIAL EFFECT ON INCOME (ALTERNATIVE 2)
Lease Equipment (Alternative 1) or Buy Equipment (Alternative 2)			

EXERCISE 24-3

a.

	Continue Star Cola (Alternative 1) or Discontinue Star Cola (Alternative 2)		
	CONTINUE STAR COLA (ALTERNATIVE 1)	DISCONTINUE STAR COLA (ALTERNATIVE 2)	DIFFERENTIAL EFFECT ON INCOME (ALTERNATIVE 2)

b. _____

_____

_____

_____

EXERCISE 24-4

a.

	CONTINUE CUPS (ALTERNATIVE 1)	DISCONTINUE CUPS (ALTERNATIVE 2)	DIFFERENTIAL EFFECT ON INCOME (ALTERNATIVE 2)

Continue Cups (Alternative 1) or Discontinue Cups (Alternative 2)

b. _____

_____

_____

_____

EXERCISE 24-5

a. _____
   _____
   _____
   _____
   _____
   _____
   _____
   _____

b. _____
   _____
   _____
   _____
   _____
   _____
   _____
   _____
   _____
   _____
   _____
   _____
   _____
   _____
   _____
   _____
   _____
   _____

c.

	INVESTOR SERVICES (IN MILLIONS)	INSTITUTIONAL SERVICES (IN MILLIONS)	

EXERCISE 24-5, Concluded

d. _____
   _____
   _____
   _____
   _____
   _____
   _____
   _____
   _____
   _____

EXERCISE 24-6

_____
_____
_____
_____
_____
_____
_____
_____
_____
_____

Continue Children's Shoes (Alternative 1) or Discontinue Children's Shoes (Alternative 2)

	CONTINUE CHILDREN'S SHOES (ALTERNATIVE 1)	DISCONTINUE CHILDREN'S SHOES (ALTERNATIVE 2)	DIFFERENTIAL EFFECT ON INCOME (ALTERNATIVE 2)

EXERCISE 24-7

a.

	Make Carrying Case (Alternative 1) or Buy Carrying Case (Alternative 2)		
	MAKE CARRYING CASE (ALTERNATIVE 1)	BUY CARRYING CASE (ALTERNATIVE 2)	DIFFERENTIAL EFFECT ON INCOME (ALTERNATIVE 2)

b. _____

_____

_____

_____

_____

_____

_____

EXERCISE 24-8

a.

	LAY OUT PAGES INTERNALLY (ALTERNATIVE 1)	PURCHASE LAYOUT SERVICES (ALTERNATIVE 2)	DIFFERENTIAL EFFECT ON INCOME (ALTERNATIVE 2)
Lay Out Pages Internally (Alternative 1) or Purchase Layout Services (Alternative 2)			

b. _____

_____

_____

_____

_____

_____

_____

EXERCISE 24-8, Concluded

c. _____

_____

_____

_____

_____

_____

_____

_____

_____

_____

_____

_____

EXERCISE 24-9

a.

	Continue with Old Machine (Alternative 1) or Replace Old Machine (Alternative 2)		

	CONTINUE WITH OLD MACHINE (ALTERNATIVE 1)	REPLACE OLD MACHINE (ALTERNATIVE 2)	DIFFERENTIAL EFFECT ON INCOME (ALTERNATIVE 2)

b. _____

_____

_____

_____

_____

_____

EXERCISE 24-10

a.

	Continue with Old Machine (Alternative 1) or Replace Old Machine (Alternative 2)		
	CONTINUE WITH OLD MACHINE (ALTERNATIVE 1)	REPLACE OLD MACHINE (ALTERNATIVE 2)	DIFFERENTIAL EFFECT ON INCOME (ALTERNATIVE 2)

b. _____
_____

c. _____
_____
_____
_____
_____
_____
_____
_____
_____
_____
_____

EXERCISE 24-11

Sell Rough Cut (Alternative 1) or Process Further into Finished Cut (Alternative 2)

	SELL ROUGH CUT (ALTERNATIVE 1)	PROCESS FURTHER INTO FINISHED CUT (ALTERNATIVE 2)	DIFFERENTIAL EFFECT ON INCOME (ALTERNATIVE 2)

EXERCISE 24-12

a.

Sell Regular Columbian (Alternative 1) or Process Further into Decaf Columbian (Alternative 2)			
	SELL REGULAR COLUMBIAN (ALTERNATIVE 1)	PROCESS FURTHER INTO DECAF COLUMBIAN (ALTERNATIVE 2)	DIFFERENTIAL EFFECT ON INCOME (ALTERNATIVE 2)

b. _____

_____

_____

_____

_____

_____

_____

EXERCISE 24-12, Concluded

c. _____

_____

_____

_____

_____

_____

_____

_____

_____

_____

_____

_____

_____

_____

_____

_____

_____

_____

_____

_____

_____

Sell Regular Columbian (Alternative 1) or Process Further into Decaf Columbian (Alternative 2)

	SELL REGULAR COLUMBIAN (ALTERNATIVE 1)	PROCESS FURTHER INTO DECAF COLUMBIAN (ALTERNATIVE 2)	DIFFERENTIAL EFFECT ON INCOME (ALTERNATIVE 2)

EXERCISE 24-13

a.

Reject Order (Alternative 1) or Accept Order (Alternative 2)			
	REJECT ORDER (ALTERNATIVE 1)	ACCEPT ORDER (ALTERNATIVE 2)	DIFFERENTIAL EFFECT ON INCOME (ALTERNATIVE 2)

b. _____

_____

_____

_____

_____

_____

_____

_____

c. _____

_____

_____

EXERCISE 24-14

_____

_____

_____

_____

EXERCISE 24-15

a.

Reject Order (Alternative 1) or Accept Order (Alternative 2)			

	REJECT ORDER (ALTERNATIVE 1)	ACCEPT ORDER (ALTERNATIVE 2)	DIFFERENTIAL EFFECT ON INCOME (ALTERNATIVE 2)

b. _____

_____

_____

_____

_____

EXERCISE 24-16

a.

b. _____

_____

_____

_____

_____

_____

_____

_____

_____

_____

_____

_____

_____

_____

_____

_____

_____

_____

EXERCISE 24-17

a. _____

b. _____

_____

c. _____

_____

_____

_____

_____

_____

_____

_____

_____

d.

EXERCISE 24-18

a. _____

b. _____

_____

c. _____

_____

_____

_____

_____

_____

_____

_____

_____

_____

_____

_____

_____

_____

EXERCISE 24-18, Concluded

d.

EXERCISE 24-19

a. _____

_____

_____

_____

_____

b. _____

_____

_____

_____

_____

_____

_____

_____

_____

_____

_____

_____

_____

_____

EXERCISE 24-20

a. _____

_____

_____

_____

_____

_____

_____

_____

_____

_____

_____

_____

_____

_____

_____

_____

b. _____

c.

_____

_____

_____

EXERCISE 24-21

	TYPE 5	TYPE 10	TYPE 20

EXERCISE 24-22

a.

	LARGE	MEDIUM	SMALL	TOTAL

b. _____

_____

	LARGE	MEDIUM	SMALL	

APPENDIX EXERCISE 24-23

a.

b.

c.

APPENDIX EXERCISE 24-24

a.

b.

c.

This Page Not Used.

PROBLEM 24-1 ___

1.

_____

_____ Operate _____ (Alternative 1) or Invest in Bonds (Alternative 2)

_____

	OPERATE _____ (ALTERNATIVE 1)	INVEST IN BONDS (ALTERNATIVE 2)	DIFFERENTIAL EFFECT ON INCOME (ALTERNATIVE 2)

2. _____

_____

3.

PROBLEM 24-2 ___

1.

	Continue with Old Machine (Alternative 1) or Replace Old Machine (Alternative 2)		

	CONTINUE WITH OLD MACHINE (ALTERNATIVE 1)	REPLACE OLD MACHINE (ALTERNATIVE 2)	DIFFERENTIAL EFFECT ON INCOME (ALTERNATIVE 2)

PROBLEM 24-2 ___, Concluded

2. _____

_____

_____

_____

_____

_____

_____

_____

_____

_____

_____

_____

_____

_____

_____

_____

_____

_____

_____

_____

_____

_____

_____

This Page Not Used.

PROBLEM 24-3 ___

1.

_____ Promote _____ (Alternative 1) or Promote _____ (Alternative 2) _____

	PROMOTE _____ _____ (ALTERNATIVE 1)	PROMOTE _____ _____ (ALTERNATIVE 2)	DIFFERENTIAL EFFECT ON INCOME (ALTERNATIVE 2)

PROBLEM 24-3 ___, Concluded

2. _____

_____

_____

_____

_____

_____

_____

_____

_____

_____

_____

_____

PROBLEM 24-4 ___

1.

Sell _____ *(Alternative 1) or Process Further into* _____ *(Alternative 2)*

	SELL _____ (ALTERNATIVE 1)	PROCESS FURTHER INTO _____ (ALTERNATIVE 2)	DIFFERENTIAL EFFECT ON INCOME (ALTERNATIVE 2)

2. _____

_____

_____

_____

_____

_____

This Page Not Used.

PROBLEM 24-5 ___

1. _____

2. a.

_____

b. _____

_____

_____

_____

_____

_____

_____

_____

_____

_____

_____

_____

_____

_____

c.

PROBLEM 24-5 ___ , Continued

3. (APPENDIX)

    a.

    b.

    c.

PROBLEM 24-5 ___, Continued

4. (APPENDIX)

a. _____

_____

_____

b. _____

_____

_____

_____

_____

_____

_____

_____

_____

_____

c.

5. _____

_____

_____

_____

_____

_____

_____

PROBLEM 24-5 ___, Concluded

6. a.

	REJECT ORDER (ALTERNATIVE 1)	ACCEPT ORDER (ALTERNATIVE 2)	DIFFERENTIAL EFFECT ON INCOME (ALTERNATIVE 2)
Reject Order (Alternative 1) or Accept Order (Alternative 2)			

b. _____

_____

PROBLEM 24-6 ___

1.

PROBLEM 24-6 ___, Concluded

2.

Explanation:

_____

_____

_____

_____

_____

_____

_____

_____

_____

_____

_____

_____

_____

_____

_____

EXERCISE 25-1

	TESTING EQUIPMENT	VEHICLE	

EXERCISE 25-2

_____

_____

_____

_____

_____

_____

_____

_____

_____

_____

_____

_____

_____

_____

_____

_____

_____

_____

_____

_____

_____

EXERCISE 25-3

_____
_____
_____
_____
_____
_____
_____
_____
_____
_____
_____
_____
_____
_____
_____
_____
_____
_____
_____
_____
_____

EXERCISE 25-4

	YEAR 1	YEARS 2–9	LAST YEAR

EXERCISE 25-5

_____

_____

_____

	NET CASH FLOW	CUMULATIVE NET CASH FLOWS

EXERCISE 25-6

a. _____

_____

_____

_____

_____

_____

	LIQUID SOAP		BODY LOTION	
	NET CASH FLOW	CUMULATIVE NET CASH FLOWS	NET CASH FLOW	CUMULATIVE NET CASH FLOWS

_____

_____

EXERCISE 25-6, Concluded

b. _____
_____
_____
_____
_____
_____
_____
_____
_____
_____
_____
_____
_____
_____

EXERCISE 25-7

a.

Year	Present Value of $1 at 15%	Net Cash Flow	Present Value of Net Cash Flow
1			
2			
3			
4			
Total...			
Less amount to be invested..			
Net present value..			

b. _____
_____
_____

EXERCISE 25-8

a.

	2016	2017	2018	2019	2020

b.

Year	Net Cash Flow [from part a.]	Present Value of $1 at 12%	Present Value of Net Cash Flow
2016			
2017			
2018			
2019			
2020			
Total present value of cash flows			
Less investment in delivery truck			
Net present value of delivery truck			

c. _____
_____
_____
_____
_____
_____

EXERCISE 25-9

a.

	(IN MILLIONS)	

EXERCISE 25-9, Concluded

b.

	(IN MILLIONS, EXCEPT PRESENT VALUE FACTOR)

c. _____

_____

_____

_____

_____

EXERCISE 25-10

a.

EXERCISE 25-10, Concluded

b.

c. _____

_____

_____

_____

d. _____

_____

_____

_____

_____

_____

_____

_____

_____

EXERCISE 25-11

a.

b.

EXERCISE 25-12

a. _____

_____

_____

_____

_____

_____

_____

_____

b. _____

_____

_____

_____

_____

_____

EXERCISE 25-13

a. _____

_____

_____

_____

_____

_____

_____

Sewing Machine:

Packing Machine:

b. _____

_____

_____

_____

_____

_____

_____

_____

_____

_____

EXERCISE 25-13, Concluded

c. _____

_____

_____

_____

_____

_____

_____

_____

_____

_____

_____

_____

_____

_____

_____

_____

_____

_____

_____

_____

EXERCISE 25-14

a. _____

_____

_____

_____

b. _____

_____

_____

c.

EXERCISE 25-15

a. _____
_____
_____

b. _____
_____
_____
_____
_____

c. _____
_____
_____
_____
_____
_____
_____
_____
_____
_____
_____
_____
_____
_____
_____
_____
_____
_____
_____
_____
_____
_____
_____
_____

EXERCISE 25-16

a. _____

_____

_____

_____

_____

_____

_____

b. _____

_____

EXERCISE 25-17

a. _____

_____

_____

_____

_____

_____

_____

_____

_____

_____

_____

_____

_____

b. _____

_____

_____

_____

_____

_____

_____

_____

_____

_____

_____

_____

_____

_____

_____

_____

_____

_____

_____

_____

_____

_____

EXERCISE 25-18

a. Delivery Truck:

Bagging Machine:

EXERCISE 25-18, Concluded

b. _____

_____

_____

_____

_____

_____

_____

_____

_____

_____

_____

_____

_____

_____

_____

_____

_____

EXERCISE 25-19

a.

b. _____

_____

c. _____

_____

_____

_____

_____

_____

_____

_____

_____

EXERCISE 25-20

_____
_____
_____
_____
_____
_____
_____
_____
_____
_____
_____
_____

EXERCISE 25-21

Processing Mill:

Year	Present Value of $1 at 15%	Net Cash Flow	Present Value of Net Cash Flow
1			
2			
3			
4			
4 (residual value)			
Total..			
Less amount to be invested...			
Net present value			

Electric Shovel:

Year	Present Value of $1 at 15%	Net Cash Flow	Present Value of Net Cash Flow
1			
2			
3			
4			
Total..			
Less amount to be invested...			
Net present value			

Conclusion with explanation:

_____

_____

_____

_____

_____

_____

_____

_____

EXERCISE 25-22

a. Blending Equipment:

Computer System:

b. _____

_____

_____

_____

_____

_____

_____

_____

_____

_____

_____

_____

PROBLEM 25-1 ___

1. a. _____

_____

_____

_____

_____

_____

_____

b.

Year	Present Value of $1 at _____%	Net Cash Flow		Present Value of Net Cash Flow	
		Project: _____ _____	Project: _____ _____	Project: _____ _____	Project: _____ _____
1					
2					
3					
4					
5					
Total............................					
Less amount to be invested...					
Net present value					

2. _____

_____

_____

_____

_____

_____

_____

_____

_____

_____

_____

_____

_____

_____

_____

_____

_____

412

This Page Not Used.

PROBLEM 25-2 ___

1. a.

Year	Net Cash Flow	Cumulative Net Cash Flow

Year	Net Cash Flow	Cumulative Net Cash Flow

b.

Year	Present Value of $1 at _____%	Net Cash Flow Project (Product): _____	Net Cash Flow Project (Product): _____	Present Value of Net Cash Flow Project (Product): _____	Present Value of Net Cash Flow Project (Product): _____
1					
2					
3					
4					
5					
Total.............................					
Less amount to be invested..					
Net present value					

PROBLEM 25-2 ___, Concluded

2. _____

_____

_____

_____

_____

_____

_____

_____

_____

_____

_____

_____

_____

_____

_____

_____

_____

_____

_____

PROBLEM 25-3 ___

1. Proposal (Project): _____

Year	Present Value of $1 at _____%	Net Cash Flow	Present Value of Net Cash Flow
1			
2			
3			
Total..			
Less amount to be invested..			
Net present value			

Proposal (Project): _____

Year	Present Value of $1 at _____%	Net Cash Flow	Present Value of Net Cash Flow
1			
2			
3			
Total..			
Less amount to be invested..			
Net present value			

Proposal (Project): _____

Year	Present Value of $1 at _____%	Net Cash Flow	Present Value of Net Cash Flow
1			
2			
3			
Total..			
Less amount to be invested..			
Net present value			

PROBLEM 25-3 ___, Concluded

2. _____

_____

_____

_____

_____

_____

_____

_____

_____

_____

_____

_____

_____

3. _____

_____

_____

_____

_____

_____

_____

_____

_____

_____

PROBLEM 25-4 ___

1. a. Project: _____

Project: _____

b. _____

_____

_____

_____

_____

_____

_____

_____

_____

_____

PROBLEM 25-4 ___, Concluded

2. a. _____

_____

_____

_____

_____

_____

_____

_____

_____

_____

_____

b. _____

_____

_____

_____

_____

3. _____

_____

_____

_____

_____

_____

_____

_____

_____

_____

_____

_____

_____

_____

_____

_____

PROBLEM 25-5 ___

1. Project (Site): _____

Project (Site): _____

2.

Year	Present Value of $1 at _____%	Net Cash Flow		Present Value of Net Cash Flow	
		Project (Site): _____	Project (Site): _____	Project (Site): _____	Project (Site): _____
1					
2					
3					
4					
4 (residual value)					
Total...............................					
Less amount to be invested...					
Net present value...					

PROBLEM 25-5 ___, Concluded

3. _____

_____

_____

_____

_____

_____

_____

_____

_____

_____

_____

_____

_____

_____

_____

_____

_____

_____

_____

_____

PROBLEM 25-6 ___

1. Proposal A:

Year	Net Cash Flow	Cumulative Net Cash Flows

Proposal B:

Year	Net Cash Flow	Cumulative Net Cash Flows

Proposal C:

Year	Net Cash Flow	Cumulative Net Cash Flows

Proposal D:

Year	Net Cash Flow	Cumulative Net Cash Flows

PROBLEM 25-6 ___, Continued

2. Proposal A: _____

_____

_____

_____

_____

_____

Proposal B: _____

_____

_____

_____

_____

_____

Proposal C: _____

_____

_____

_____

_____

_____

Proposal D: _____

_____

_____

_____

_____

_____

PROBLEM 25-6 ___, Continued

3.

Proposal	Cash Payback Period	Average Rate of Return	Accept for Further Analysis	Reject
A				
B				
C				
D				

4. Proposal ___:

Year	Present Value of $1 at _____%	Net Cash Flow	Present Value of Net Cash Flow
1			
2			
3			
4			
5			
Total..			
Less amount to be invested...		
Net present value		

Proposal ___:

Year	Present Value of $1 at _____%	Net Cash Flow	Present Value of Net Cash Flow
1			
2			
3			
4			
5			
Total..			
Less amount to be invested...		
Net present value		

PROBLEM 25-6 ___, Concluded

5. _____

6. _____

7. _____

8. _____

EXERCISE 26-1

_____

_____

EXERCISE 26-2

a. _____

_____

_____

_____

_____

Supporting calculations:

b.

EXERCISE 26-3

a. _____

_____

_____

_____

_____

Supporting calculations:

b.

EXERCISE 26-4

a.

_____
_____
_____
_____
_____

b.

EXERCISE 26-4, Concluded

c.

	PISTONS	VALVES	CAMS
Product Line Budgeted Gross Profit Reports			

d. _____

_____

_____

_____

_____

EXERCISE 26-5

a.

	PATTERN DEPARTMENT	CUT AND SEW DEPARTMENT

b. Small Glove:

Medium Glove:

Large Glove:

EXERCISE 26-6

a. _____

b.

	ASSEMBLY DEPARTMENT	TESTING DEPARTMENT

Commercial Motor:

Residential Motor:

EXERCISE 26-6, Concluded

c. _____
_____
_____
_____
_____
_____
_____
_____
_____
_____
_____
_____
_____
_____
_____
_____
_____
_____
_____
_____
_____

EXERCISE 26-7

a. _____
_____
_____
_____
_____

EXERCISE 26-7, Continued

b.

	FABRICATION DEPARTMENT	ASSEMBLY DEPARTMENT	

Gasoline Engine:

Diesel Engine:

EXERCISE 26-7, Concluded

c. _____

_____

_____

_____

_____

_____

_____

_____

_____

_____

_____

_____

_____

_____

_____

_____

_____

_____

_____

_____

_____

_____

_____

_____

_____

EXERCISE 26-8

Activity	Activity Base
Accounting reports	
Customer return processing.........................	
Electric power..	
Human resources..	
Inventory control...	
Invoice and collecting..................................	
Machine depreciation...................................	
Materials handling..	
Order shipping..	
Payroll	
Production control	
Production setup	
Purchasing	
Quality control	
Sales order processing	

EXERCISE 26-9

a. Sales order processing activity rate: _____

_____

b. Sales order processing cost: _____

_____

EXERCISE 26-10

	A	B	C	D	E	F	G	H	I	J	K
			Elliptical Machines						Treadmills		
1											
2											
3											
4											
5											
6											
7											
8											
9											
10											
11											
12											
13											
14											
15											

EXERCISE 26-11

a.

	A	B	C	D	E	F
1						
2						
3						
4						
5						
6						
7						
8						

EXERCISE 26-11, Concluded

b.

	A	B	C	D	E	F	G	H	I	J	K
			Entry Lighting Fixtures					Dining Room Lighting Fixtures			
1											
2											
3											
4											
5											
6											
7											
8											
9											
10											
11											
12											
13											
14											
15											

EXERCISE 26-12

a.

	A	B	Procurement	C	Scheduling	D	Materials Handling	E	Product Development
1									
2									
3									
4									
5									

EXERCISE 26-12, Concluded

b.

	A	B	C	D	E	F	G	H	I	J	K
				Ovens					Refrigerators		
1											
2											
3											
4											
5											
6											
7											
8											
9											
10											
11											
12											
13											
14											
15											

EXERCISE 26-13

a. _____

_____

_____

_____

_____

b.

	SETUP	PRODUCTION SUPPORT	

EXERCISE 26-13, Continued

c.

	A	B	C	D	E	F	G	H	I	J	K
				Cell Phones					Tablets		
1											
2											
3											
4											
5											
6											
7											
8											
9											
10											
11											
12											

EXERCISE 26-13, Concluded

d. _____

_____

_____

_____

_____

_____

_____

_____

_____

_____

_____

_____

_____

_____

_____

_____

_____

_____

_____

_____

EXERCISE 26-14

a.

	ASSEMBLY DEPARTMENT	TEST AND PACK DEPARTMENT

EXERCISE 26-14, Concluded

b.

	A	B	C	D	E	F	G	H	I	J	K
				Blender					Toaster Oven		
1											
2											
3											
4											
5											
6											
7											
8											
9											
10											
11											
12											

EXERCISE 26-15

a.

	ASSEMBLY ACTIVITY	TEST AND PACK ACTIVITY	SETUP ACTIVITY	

EXERCISE 26-15, Concluded

b.

	A	B	C	D	E	F	G	H	I	J	K
				Blender					Toaster Oven		
1											
2											
3											
4											
5											
6											
7											
8											
9											
10											
11											
12											

EXERCISE 26-16

a.

Product Volume Class	Column A Single Rate Overhead Allocation per Unit	Column B ABC Overhead Allocation per Unit	Column C Percent Change in Allocation (Col. B – Col. A) ÷ Col. A
Low			
Medium			
High			

Calculations:

_____

_____

_____

_____

_____

_____

_____

_____

_____

_____

_____

_____

b. _____

_____

_____

_____

_____

_____

_____

_____

_____

_____

_____

_____

EXERCISE 26-16, Concluded

c. _____

_____

_____

_____

_____

_____

_____

_____

_____

_____

_____

_____

_____

_____

_____

_____

_____

_____

_____

_____

_____

_____

_____

_____

EXERCISE 26-17

_____
_____
_____
_____
_____
_____
_____
_____
_____
_____
_____
_____
_____
_____
_____
_____
_____
_____

EXERCISE 26-18

a. Sales order processing activities:

Post-sale customer service activities:

EXERCISE 26-18, Continued

b.

	GENERATORS	AIR COMPRESSORS	TOTAL
Product Profitability Report			

EXERCISE 26-18, Concluded

c. _____

_____

_____

_____

_____

_____

_____

_____

_____

_____

_____

_____

_____

_____

_____

_____

_____

_____

_____

_____

_____

_____

EXERCISE 26-19

a.

	CUSTOMER 1	CUSTOMER 2	CUSTOMER 3

Customer Profitability Report

(assumed data)

EXERCISE 26-19, Concluded

b. _____

_____

_____

_____

_____

_____

_____

_____

_____

_____

_____

_____

_____

_____

EXERCISE 26-20

a.

	A	B	C	D	E	F	G	H	I	J	K
				Patient Putin					Patient Umit		
1											
2											
3											
4											
5											
6											
7											
8											
9											
10											

b.

EXERCISE 26-21

a.

Product Profitability Report			
	AUTO	WORKERS' COMP.	HOMEOWNERS

EXERCISE 26-21, Concluded

b. _____

_____

_____

_____

_____

_____

_____

_____

_____

_____

_____

_____

_____

_____

_____

_____

_____

_____

_____

_____

_____

_____

PROBLEM 26-1 ___

1. a. Using direct labor hours: _____

_____

_____

_____

_____

b. Using machine hours: _____

_____

_____

_____

_____

2. a. Using the direct labor hour plantwide factory overhead rate:

b. Using the machine hour plantwide factory overhead rate:

This Page Not Used.

PROBLEM 26-2 ___

1.

	DEPARTMENT	DEPARTMENT	

2. _____

This Page Not Used.

PROBLEM 26-3 ___

1.

	DEPARTMENT	DEPARTMENT	

2.

PROBLEM 26-3 ___, Continued

3.

PROBLEM 26-3 ____, Continued

4.

	A	B	C	D	E	F	G	H	I	J	K
1											
2											
3											
4											
5											
6											
7											
8											
9											
10											
11											
12											
13											
14											
15											

PROBLEM 26-3 ___, Concluded

5. _____

_____

_____

_____

_____

_____

_____

_____

_____

_____

_____

_____

_____

_____

_____

_____

_____

PROBLEM 26-4 _____

1.

PROBLEM 26-4 ____, Continued

2.

	A	B	C	D	E	F	G	H	I	J	K
1											
2											
3											
4											
5											
6											
7											
8											
9											
10											
11											
12											
13											
14											
15											

PROBLEM 26-4 ___, Concluded

	A	B	C	D	E	F
1						
2						
3						
4						
5						
6						
7						
8						
9						
10						
11						
12						
13						
14						
15						

3. _____

_____

_____

_____

_____

_____

_____

_____

_____

_____

_____

This Page Not Used.

PROBLEM 26-5 ___

1.

2. _____

PROBLEM 26-5 ___, Continued

3.

	Customer Profitability Report		

PROBLEM 26-5 ___, Concluded

4. _____

_____

_____

_____

_____

_____

_____

_____

_____

_____

_____

_____

_____

_____

_____

_____

_____

_____

_____

_____

_____

_____

_____

_____

_____

_____

_____

_____

_____

_____

_____

_____

_____

_____

_____

_____

_____

This Page Not Used.

PROBLEM 26-6 ___

1.

_____

_____

_____

_____

_____

_____

_____

_____

PROBLEM 26-6 ___, Continued

2.

PROBLEM 26-6 ___, Continued

3.

PROBLEM 26-6 ___ , Concluded

4. _____

_____

_____

_____

_____

_____

_____

_____

_____

_____

_____

_____

_____

_____

_____

_____

_____

_____

_____

_____

_____

_____

_____

_____

_____

_____

_____

_____

_____

EXERCISE 27-1

_____
_____
_____
_____
_____
_____
_____
_____
_____
_____
_____
_____
_____
_____
_____
_____
_____
_____
_____
_____
_____
_____
_____
_____
_____
_____

EXERCISE 27-2

_____
_____
_____
_____
_____
_____
_____
_____
_____
_____
_____
_____
_____
_____
_____
_____
_____
_____
_____
_____
_____
_____
_____
_____
_____
_____
_____
_____
_____
_____
_____

EXERCISE 27-3

_____

_____

_____

_____

_____

_____

_____

_____

_____

_____

_____

_____

_____

_____

_____

_____

_____

_____

_____

_____

_____

_____

_____

_____

_____

_____

_____

_____

_____

_____

_____

EXERCISE 27-4

_____
_____
_____
_____
_____
_____
_____
_____
_____
_____
_____
_____
_____
_____

EXERCISE 27-5

a. _____
_____
_____
_____
_____
_____
_____
_____
_____
_____
_____
_____
_____
_____

EXERCISE 27-5, Concluded

b. _____

_____

_____

_____

_____

_____

_____

_____

_____

_____

_____

_____

_____

_____

_____

_____

_____

_____

_____

_____

_____

_____

_____

_____

_____

_____

_____

_____

c.

EXERCISE 27-6

Traditional Philosophy

	VALUE-ADDED TIME	NON-VALUE-ADDED TIME	TOTAL TIME

_____

_____

_____

_____

_____

Just-in-Time Philosophy

	VALUE-ADDED TIME	NON-VALUE-ADDED TIME	TOTAL TIME

_____

_____

_____

_____

_____

EXERCISE 27-7

Present Approach

	VALUE-ADDED TIME	NON-VALUE-ADDED TIME	TOTAL TIME

Proposed Approach

	VALUE-ADDED TIME	NON-VALUE-ADDED TIME	TOTAL TIME

EXERCISE 27-8

a. and b.

Elapsed Time (a)	Activity	Value-Added Time	Non-Value-Added Time (b)
1:00 P.M.	Arrives at doctor's office		
_____ P.M.			
_____ P.M.			
_____ P.M.			
_____ P.M.			
_____ P.M.			
_____ P.M.			
_____ P.M.			
_____ P.M.			
_____ P.M.			
	Total		

Simmons arrives home at _____.

b. _____

_____

_____

c. _____

_____

_____

_____

_____

EXERCISE 27-8, Concluded

d. _____

_____

_____

_____

_____

_____

_____

_____

_____

_____

_____

_____

_____

_____

_____

_____

_____

_____

_____

_____

_____

_____

_____

_____

_____

EXERCISE 27-9

a. _____

b. _____

EXERCISE 27-9, Concluded

c. _____

_____

_____

_____

_____

_____

_____

_____

_____

_____

_____

_____

_____

_____

_____

_____

_____

EXERCISE 27-10

EXERCISE 27-11

_____
_____
_____
_____
_____
_____
_____
_____
_____
_____
_____
_____
_____
_____
_____
_____
_____
_____
_____
_____
_____
_____
_____
_____
_____
_____
_____
_____
_____
_____
_____
_____

EXERCISE 27-12

a. _____

_____

_____

_____

_____

_____

_____

_____

_____

_____

_____

_____

_____

EXERCISE 27-12, Concluded

b. _____

_____

_____

_____

_____

_____

_____

_____

_____

_____

_____

_____

_____

_____

_____

_____

_____

_____

_____

_____

_____

_____

_____

_____

_____

_____

_____

_____

_____

_____

_____

_____

_____

_____

_____

_____

EXERCISE 27-13

EXERCISE 27-14

a. _____

_____

_____

_____

_____

b. _____

_____

_____

_____

_____

_____

_____

EXERCISE 27-14, Concluded

c. (1) through (4)

JOURNAL

PAGE _____

	DATE		DESCRIPTION	POST. REF.	DEBIT	CREDIT	
1							1
2							2
3							3
4							4
5							5
6							6
7							7
8							8
9							9
10							10
11							11
12							12
13							13
14							14
15							15
16							16
17							17
18							18
19							19
20							20
21							21
22							22
23							23
24							24
25							25
26							26
27							27
28							28

EXERCISE 27-15

a. _____
   _____
   _____
   _____
   _____

b. _____
   _____
   _____
   _____
   _____
   _____
   _____

EXERCISE 27-15, Concluded

c. (1) through (4)

JOURNAL

	DATE		DESCRIPTION	POST. REF.	DEBIT	CREDIT	
1							1
2							2
3							3
4							4
5							5
6							6
7							7
8							8
9							9
10							10
11							11
12							12
13							13
14							14
15							15
16							16
17							17
18							18
19							19
20							20
21							21
22							22
23							23
24							24
25							25
26							26
27							27
28							28

EXERCISE 27-16

a. (1) through (4)

	DATE		DESCRIPTION	POST. REF.	DEBIT	CREDIT	
1							1
2							2
3							3
4							4
5							5
6							6
7							7
8							8
9							9
10							10
11							11
12							12
13							13
14							14
15							15
16							16
17							17
18							18
19							19
20							20
21							21
22							22
23							23
24							24
25							25
26							26
27							27
28							28

JOURNAL PAGE

EXERCISE 27-16, Concluded

b.

Supporting calculations:

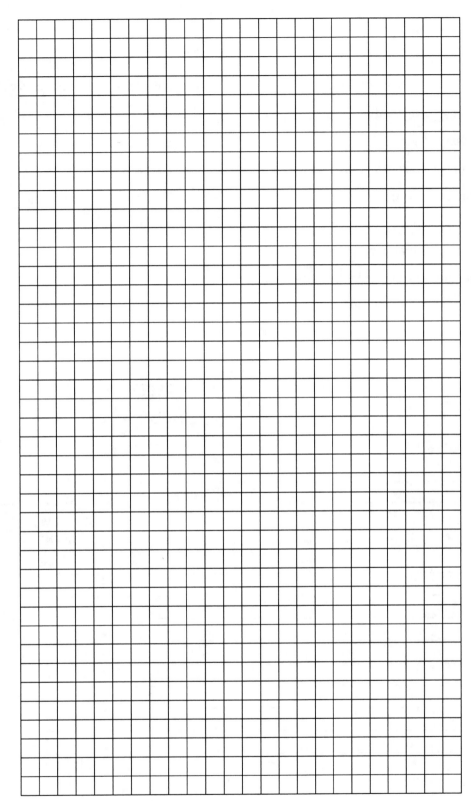

Pareto Chart of Quality Activities

Dollars

EXERCISE 27-17

EXERCISE 27-18

a.

Quality Activities	Activity Cost	Quality Cost Classification
Correct shipment errors	$144,000	
Disposing of scrap......................................	90,000	
Emergency equipment maintenance	99,000	
Employee training	36,000	
Final inspection	81,000	
Inspecting incoming materials...................	54,000	
Preventive equipment maintenance..........	27,000	
Processing customer returns	90,000	
Scrap reporting..	36,000	
Supplier development	9,000	
Warranty claims	234,000	
Total	$900,000	

b.

	Cost of Quality Report		

	COST SUMMARY		
QUALITY COST CLASSIFICATION	QUALITY COST	PERCENT OF TOTAL QUALITY COST	PERCENT OF TOTAL SALES

EXERCISE 27-18, Concluded

c. _____

_____

_____

_____

_____

_____

_____

_____

_____

_____

_____

_____

_____

EXERCISE 27-19

Pareto Chart of Quality Activities

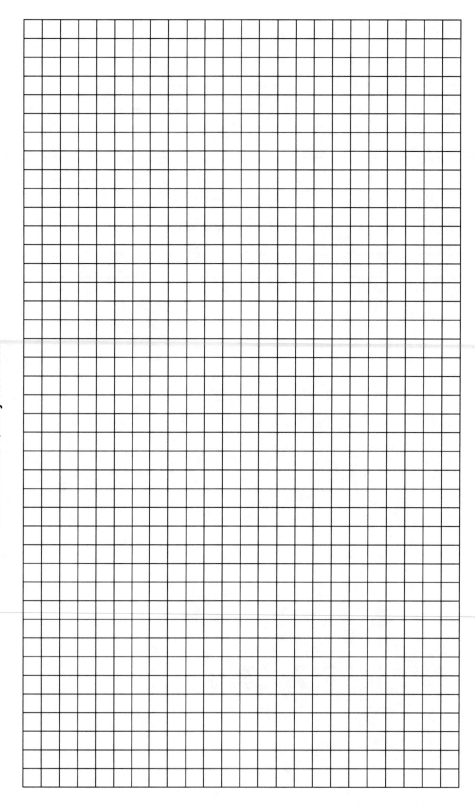

Dollars

EXERCISE 27-20

a.

Quality Activities	Activity Cost	Quality Cost Classification	Value-Added/ Non-Value Added
Billing error correction.......	$ 36,000		
Cable signal testing...........	96,000		
Reinstalling service (installed incorrectly the first time)	30,000		
Repairing satellite equipment	36,000		
Repairing underground cable connections to the customer	18,000		
Replacing old technology cable with higher quality cable	168,000		
Replacing old technology signal switches with higher quality switches....	126,000		
Responding to customer home repair requests......	24,000		
Training employees...........	66,000		
Total	$600,000		

b.

Cost of Quality Report			
	COST SUMMARY		
QUALITY COST CLASSIFICATION	QUALITY COST	PERCENT OF TOTAL QUALITY COST	PERCENT OF TOTAL SALES

EXERCISE 27-20, Concluded

c.

CATEGORY	AMOUNT	PERCENT	

Value-Added/Non-Value-Added Activity Analysis

d. _____

_____

_____

_____

_____

_____

_____

_____

_____

_____

_____

EXERCISE 27-21

a. _____

_____

_____

_____

_____

_____

b. _____

_____

_____

_____

_____

_____

Calculations:

_____

_____

_____

_____

_____

_____

EXERCISE 27-21, Concluded

c. _____

_____

_____

_____

_____

_____

_____

_____

_____

_____

_____

_____

_____

_____

_____

_____

_____

_____

_____

_____

EXERCISE 27-22

a.

ACTIVITY	COST	PERCENT OF TOTAL PROCESS

b. _____

_____

_____

c.

ACTIVITY	ACTIVITY COST PRIOR TO IMPROVEMENT	ACTIVITY COST AFTER IMPROVEMENT	ACTIVITY COST SAVINGS (COST)

d. _____

_____

_____

EXERCISE 27-23

a.

ACTIVITY	COST	PERCENT OF TOTAL PROCESS

b. _____

_____

_____

EXERCISE 27-23, Concluded

c.

ACTIVITY	ACTIVITY COST PRIOR TO IMPROVEMENT	ACTIVITY COST AFTER IMPROVEMENT	ACTIVITY COST SAVINGS

d. _____

_____

_____

This Page Not Used.

PROBLEM 27-1 ___

1. _____

_____

_____

_____

_____

_____

_____

_____

_____

_____

_____

_____

_____

_____

_____

_____

_____

_____

_____

_____

_____

_____

_____

_____

PROBLEM 27-1 ___ , Continued

2. _____

_____

_____

_____

_____

_____

_____

_____

_____

_____

_____

_____

_____

_____

_____

_____

_____

_____

_____

_____

_____

_____

_____

_____

_____

PROBLEM 27-1 ___, Concluded

3. _____

_____

_____

_____

_____

_____

_____

514

This Page Not Used.

PROBLEM 27-2 ___

1. Value-added time:

Non-value-added time:

Value-added ratio:

_____

_____

_____

_____

_____

PROBLEM 27-2 ___, Concluded

2. _____

_____

_____

_____

_____

_____

_____

_____

_____

_____

_____

_____

_____

_____

_____

_____

_____

_____

PROBLEM 27-3 ___

1. _____

   _____

   _____

   _____

   _____

2. _____

   _____

   _____

   _____

   _____

PROBLEM 27-3 ___, Continued

3. (a) through (d)

JOURNAL

	DATE	DESCRIPTION	POST. REF.	DEBIT	CREDIT	
1						1
2						2
3						3
4						4
5						5
6						6
7						7
8						8
9						9
10						10
11						11
12						12
13						13
14						14
15						15
16						16
17						17
18						18
19						19
20						20
21						21
22						22
23						23
24						24
25						25
26						26
27						27
28						28

PROBLEM 27-3 ___, Concluded

4. _____

_____

_____

_____

_____

_____

_____

5. _____

_____

_____

_____

_____

_____

_____

_____

_____

_____

_____

_____

_____

_____

_____

_____

_____

_____

_____

_____

_____

This Page Not Used.

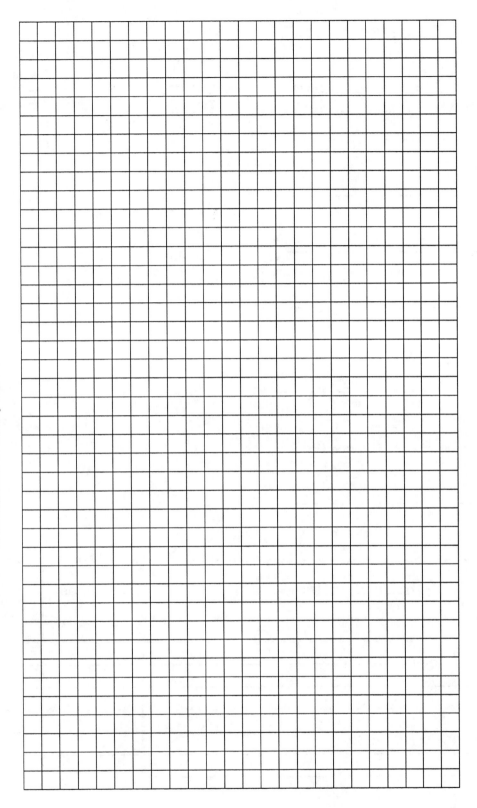

Pareto Chart of Quality Activities

Dollars

PROBLEM 27-4

1.

PROBLEM 27-4 ___, Continued

2.

Activity	Activity Cost	Cost of Quality Classification	Value-Added/ Non-Value Added Classification
_____	_____		
_____	_____		
_____	_____		
_____	_____		
_____	_____		
_____	_____		
_____	_____		
_____	_____		
_____	_____		
_____	_____		
_____	_____		
_____	_____		

3.

QUALITY COST CLASSIFICATION	ACTIVITY COST	PERCENT OF TOTAL DEPARTMENT COST

PROBLEM 27-4 ___, Concluded

4.

	ACTIVITY COST	PERCENT OF TOTAL DEPARTMENT COST	

5. _____

_____

_____

_____

_____

_____

_____

_____

_____

_____

_____

_____

This Page Not Used.

CPSIA information can be obtained
at www.ICGtesting.com
Printed in the USA
FFOW02n1049310316
22840FF